SWIFTER, HIGHER, STRONGER

A PHOTOGRAPHIC HISTORY OF
THE SUMMER OLYMPICS

On a clear summer night in 1992, the Olympic flame dominates the horizon of Barcelona, Spain.

SWIFTER, HIGHER, STRONGER

A PHOTOGRAPHIC HISTORY OF
THE SUMMER OLYMPICS

BY SUE MACY • FOREWORD BY BOB COSTAS

WASHINGTON, D.C.

FOR MY BROTHER, BERNARD "BUDDY" MACY, WHO STILL
DREAMS OF WINNING THE GOLD MEDAL IN TABLE TENNIS

ACKNOWLEDGMENTS

*Thanks to the staff of the sports library at the Amateur Athletic Foundation of Los Angeles for their help
in wrestling with Olympic data, searching for photographs, and finding my way around their amazing
facility. Special appreciation goes to Karen Goddy, assistant treasurer, and Wayne Wilson, vice president
of research and information. For their assistance with photo research, thanks to the always supportive
Grace How, as well as Karina Kabigting of Corbis, the staff of Getty Images, and Mike LeTourneau
of AP/Wide World. Once again, the folks at National Geographic—Nancy Feresten, Jennifer Emmett,
Janet Dustin, Marty Ittner, and Marfé Ferguson Delano in particular—provided much encouragement
and inspiration. A final thanks goes to my 12th-grade gym teacher, Elizabeth Sobel. Years ago, Mrs. Sobel
indulged my dire fear of the balance beam by letting me skip a day on that apparatus and write an article
about the importance of the Olympics instead. Little did she know what she started!—SM*

FRONT COVER: SWIMMING PHENOM
MICHAEL PHELPS OF THE U.S. IS
ON HIS WAY TO A GOLD MEDAL IN
THE 200-METER INDIVIDUAL MEDLEY
AT THE 2004 SUMMER OLYMPICS.
PHELPS WOULD WIN A TOTAL OF
SIX GOLD AND TWO BRONZE MEDALS
IN ATHENS, MAKING HIM ONLY
THE SECOND ATHLETE EVER TO
TAKE HOME EIGHT MEDALS FROM
A SINGLE OLYMPIAD. SOVIET
GYMNAST ALEKSANDR DITYATIN
DID IT FIRST, IN 1980.

BACK COVER: BLYTHE HARTLEY OF
CANADA SHOWS THE FORM THAT
WON HER A PLACE IN THE FINALS
OF THE 3-METER SPRINGBOARD
DIVING COMPETITION AT THE 2004
OLYMPICS. SHE FINISHED FIFTH.
ALSO AT ATHENS, GYMNAST ERIC
LOPEZ RIOS OF CUBA COMPETES
IN THE MEN'S INDIVIDUAL ALL-
AROUND FINAL. HE FINISHED 20TH.
BACKGROUND: CHIEL WARNERS OF
THE NETHERLANDS THROWS THE DIS-
CUS ON THE WAY TO A FIFTH-PLACE
FINISH IN THE DECATHLON IN 2004.

Book design is by Marty Ittner.
The body text of the book is set in Scala.
The display text is set in Base 9 SC.

Published with permission from the United States Olympic
Committee and the International Olympic Committee.

Library of Congress Cataloging-in-Publication Data
Macy, Sue.
   Swifter, higher, stronger : a photographic history of the Summer
Olympics / by Sue Macy.
      p. cm.
Summary: A detailed look at the history of the Olympic Games,
from their origins in Ancient Greece, through their rebirth in nine-
teenth century France, to the present, highlighting the contribu-
tions of individuals to their success and popularity.
      Includes bibliographical references and index.
1. Olympics—History. 2. Olympics—History—Pictorial works.
[1. Olympics—History.] I. Title.
GV721.5 .M25 2004
796.48'022'2—dc22

                              2003014079

Hardcover ISBN: 978-1-4263-0290-9
Library Edition ISBN: 978-1-4263-0302-9

Printed in Mexico

CONTENTS

Olympic
Torch,
1960
Summer
Games

THESE 44 WORDS, known as the Olympic creed, give the Olympic Games special purpose and significance.

It's hard to find an athletic honor greater than Olympic champion. Still, many competitors take to the track, or pool, or court, with no chance of earning a medal. They find fulfillment in representing their nation, in challenging themselves against the best, in exceeding their personal records, in experiencing a moment for which they waited four years or more.

For most Olympic athletes, preparation is a test of character, as they toil in relative solitude with little, if any, financial support. They stay dedicated and determined, their eyes on a goal so far down the road as to be barely visible. And when their day finally comes, they step out of obscurity's shadows and into the brightest spotlight imaginable, where there's no room for a mistake, an injury, a bad break. At the Olympics, it can literally be now or never.

It's no surprise, then, that the Games have produced so much high drama and athletic brilliance. I think of Lake Placid and Team USA's miraculous ice hockey upset of the Soviets in 1980. Or Michael Johnson's electrifying world-record shattering sprint to glory in the 200 meters at the 1996 Atlanta Games.

Sometimes, the meaning of the Olympics goes beyond sports. In 1936, with Adolf Hitler turning the Berlin Games into a Nazi showcase, African-American Jesse Owens ran and jumped to four golds, all the while carrying himself with great grace in the face of racism and hatred. In 1956, weeks after the Soviet Union crushed a revolution in Hungary, athletes from those nations met in a water polo match that saw the pool turn red with blood, as the Hungarians asserted national pride with a stirring victory.

Most notable and tragic was the murder of 11 Israelis by Palestinian terrorists at the 1972 Munich Games. Despite their lofty ideals, the Olympics are never free of politics or unaffected by the world's troubles.

In many ways the Olympics are an education. After all, they date back to 776 B.C. If geography and culture are your interests, consider the fact that upwards of 200 nations gather at the Summer Games. We learn about host cities that for two weeks become the sports capitals of the world. And athletes themselves offer

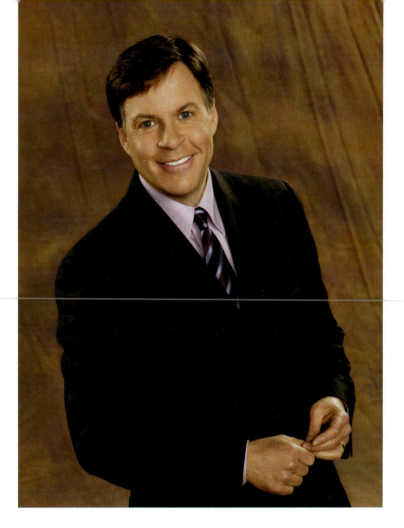

BOB COSTAS JOINED NBC SPORTS IN 1979
AND HAS SERVED AS THE PRIME-TIME HOST
FOR ALL OF THE NETWORK'S BROADCASTS OF
THE OLYMPIC GAMES SINCE 1992. THE WINNER
OF 19 EMMY AWARDS, COSTAS HAS COVERED
EVERY MAJOR SPORT FOR NBC. SINCE 2001,
HE ALSO HAS HOSTED SEVERAL SPORTS AND
INTERVIEW PROGRAMS ON HBO.

FOREWORD
BY BOB COSTAS

a glimpse into the soul and spirit of their homelands. We remember the torpedo-like Ian Thorpe of waterbound Australia, powering through the pool to multiple medals in Sydney; or the graceful Abebe Bikila of impoverished Ethiopia, running barefoot through the streets of Rome toward marathon gold; or the indomitable women of Norway's soccer team, coming back after losing to the U.S. in the early rounds of the 2000 Olympics, only to beat them, in overtime, in the final.

Also part of the Olympics' appeal is the wide variety of events demanding everything from blurring speed, to flawless precision, to Herculean strength, unwavering poise, and sometimes a combination of all four. And there are always the stories that truly inspire, such as Wilma Rudolph, conquering polio first by shedding her leg braces as a child, then by sprinting to triple-gold in Rome in 1960.

For all these reasons and more, the Olympics continue to command our attention, capture our imaginations, and inspire those of us who cover them to share their abundant flavor and excitement with the world.

WHEN I WAS 14 YEARS OLD, I dreamed of becoming an Olympic volleyball player. At the time, there were few high-profile opportunities for women to compete in sports. Volleyball was the first women's team sport at the Olympics, and I had learned to love the game at camp. In my 1968 diary, I boldly stated my intention of making the next U.S. team in 1972.

Alas, that never happened. But as I grew older, I continued to dream of Olympic glory, this time in swimming. I swam for exercise about an hour a day, three times a week. As my arms sliced through the water, I imagined that I was Donna de Varona, or Shirley Babashoff, or later, Janet Evans. Every time I swam I knew that I was getting stronger. My mind made the leap that my body would never make, from a lap pool in New Jersey to the Olympic venues of Tokyo, Montreal, and Seoul.

In 1968 the Olympics were a smaller and more intimate affair, with 5,530 athletes competing at the Summer Games, only 780 of them female. (At Athens

in 2004 there were 10,625 athletes, 4,329 of them female.) Olympic TV coverage was in its infancy, too. The 1968 Mexico City Games were only the third Summer Olympiad to be broadcast worldwide, and the increased presence of TV concerned some officials. They warned that this new visibility would change the very nature of the Games. Indeed, my diary from that year includes an account of the protest by Tommie Smith and John Carlos, two African-American athletes who raised their fists in a Black Power salute while receiving their medals in the 200-meter run. By broadcasting that image

DISCUS SPECIALIST AL OERTER (ABOVE) WAS THE FIRST ATHLETE TO WIN GOLD MEDALS IN THE SAME TRACK AND FIELD EVENT FOUR CONSECUTIVE TIMES. HE SET A NEW OLYMPIC RECORD WITH EACH WINNING THROW. AFTER RETIRING FROM COMPETITION, DONNA DE VARONA (LEFT) BECAME A TV SPORTSCASTER AND AN ADVOCATE FOR FEMALE ATHLETES. SHE CHAIRED THE HIGHLY SUCCESSFUL 1999 WOMEN'S WORLD CUP.

INTRODUCTION

around the world, TV helped to cement the status of the Olympic Games as a forum for political expression.

TV also gave personalities to the often anonymous athletes who we saw on the world stage every four years. Through "up close and personal" profiles, we grew to care whether American Al Oerter won his fourth gold medal in the discus throw in 1968 (he did), and whether Vitaly Scherbo of Belarus won four gymnastics medals in one day in 1992 (he did). TV made the competitors seem more human and our relationship with them more intimate. It introduced us to instant role models who we could imagine emulating in our own sports fantasies.

Today, the Olympic Games are an enormous institution, with their fair share of excitement and controversy, triumph and scandal. This book will look at how they got that way. But it will also highlight stories of the dynamic athletes whose personal achievements are etched in history. When it comes right down to it, that's really what the Olympic Games are all about.

South Korea's ★ JANG YONG-HO ★ helps his country win the men's team gold medal in archery at the 2000 Olympic Games. South Korean women would take the gold in both the team and individual events in that sport at Sydney.

Twin brothers ★ PAVOL HOCHSCHORNER ★ (left) and ★ PETER HOCHSCHORNER ★ of Slovakia show their form on the way to a gold medal in the canoe slalom doubles at the 2000 Summer Olympics in Sydney, Australia.

Boxing gloves used by Olympics founder Pierre de Coubertin

★ FLORIN VLAD ★ (above) of Romania shows the strain of trying to lift 105 kilograms (231 pounds) at the 2000 Sydney Games. Vlad would not finish in medal contention.

British boxer ★ FREDERICK GRACE ★ (shown here) beat his countryman, F. Frederick Spiller, to win the lightweight boxing crown at the 1908 Olympics in London.

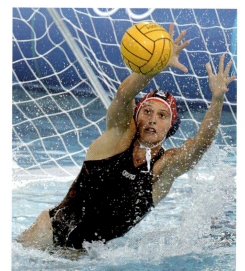

Goalkeeper ★ GEORGIA ELLINAKI ★ of Italy stops a shot on goal by Greece during the gold-medal match in water polo at the 2004 Olympics. Italy took the gold with a 10–9 victory.

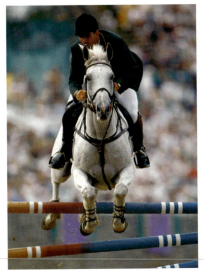

★ **Alvaro Alfonso de Miranda Neto** ★ helps Brazil take the bronze medal in the team jumping equestrian event at the 1996 Summer Games.

Swimmers gracefully take off at the start of the 100-meter backstroke final at the 2000 Olympic Games. ★ **Lenny Krayzelburg** ★ of the U.S. (third from bottom) would edge out Australia's ★ **Matthew Welsh** ★ (second from bottom) for the gold.

COMPETING

★ **Mary Lou Retton** ★ of the U.S. performs a flip on the balance beam at the 1984 Olympic Games. Retton became the first American woman to win an individual Olympic medal in gymnastics when she took the gold medal in the individual all-around event.

★ **Hadi Saei Bonehkohal** ★ of Iran (right) defends against a roundhouse kick from ★ **Huang Chih Hsuing** ★ of Chinese Taipei in the gold medal match in men's 58-68 kilogram tae kwon do at Athens. The Iranian would take the gold.

Princeton student Robert Garrett couldn't find a discus to practice with anywhere in the U.S., so his professor had one made based on a description in a history book. When Garrett arrived in Athens for the 1896 Olympics, he learned that his discus was five times as heavy as a standard one. He threw the lighter model seven and a half inches farther than anyone else and won the event. Top, an early wooden Olympic discus

PIERRE DE COUBERTIN WAS A SMALL MAN with a shrill voice and a bushy mustache, hardly the traditional image of an athlete. A French newspaper once called him "a literary type who reserves all his strength for mental matters." In fact, Coubertin was an avid sportsman, taking part in boxing, horseback riding, fencing, and rowing well into his later years. But one would scarcely imagine by looking

THE GAMES
REBORN

at him that Coubertin would almost single-handedly bring the modern Olympic Games to life and carry their fate on his shoulders.

Coubertin was born into a wealthy family in Paris in 1863. He rejected his parents' suggestions that he enter politics or the military and instead became an educator. Through his athletic pursuits, Coubertin came to believe that sports had the power to instill moral character in young men. For that reason, he was convinced that sports should be an essential part of the school curriculum. In the late 1880s, he undertook a research project to learn the exact nature of the physical education programs at every high school in France.

ALTHOUGH HE DIED OF A HEART
ATTACK ON SEPTEMBER 2, 1937,
PIERRE DE COUBERTIN CONTINUES
TO BE AN ONGOING PRESENCE AT
THE OLYMPIC GAMES. ACCORDING
TO HIS WISHES, HE WAS BURIED
IN LAUSANNE, SWITZERLAND, HOME
OF THE INTERNATIONAL OLYMPIC
COMMITTEE. BUT HIS HEART WAS
TAKEN TO OLYMPIA, GREECE, AND
BURIED IN A MONUMENT THERE.
IT IS THE FIRST STOP IN THE TORCH
RELAY THAT LEADS UP TO EACH
STAGING OF THE OLYMPIC GAMES.

While he was working on this survey, Coubertin began to read about the efforts of German archaeologists to unearth the ruins of ancient Greece. He became fascinated with accounts of the ancient Olympic Games, held every four years from 776 B.C. to A.D. 393. "Perfect equality prevailed at these games," Coubertin read in a history of Greece published in 1887. "Neither birth not fortune gave any man advantage. All, whether rich or poor, obscure or noble, might enter."

Coubertin learned that in the beginning, the ancient Olympics consisted of one race, a sprint of about 200 meters. Other events were added over the years, including boxing, wrestling, chariot racing, and a pentathlon made up of a sprint race, javelin and discus throws, wrestling, and the long jump. For the first 400 years of the Olympics, only men competed. After that, some women were allowed to enter. The Games got their name from Olympia, the valley in southwestern Greece where they took place.

At the same time that Coubertin immersed himself in the history of the ancient Olympics, he became interested in the impact of the World's Fairs, or Expositions, that were held in Paris in 1878 and 1889. These festivals highlighted advances in science and architecture, art and culture. The now-famous Eiffel Tower was built for the 1889 Universal Exposition, which celebrated the growing use of electricity as the most dramatic advance of the decade. That festival also included exhibits focusing on life on the Asian and African continents, complete with natives who introduced visitors to their foods, crafts, and customs.

More than 32 million people visited the 1889 Exposition, which included an opening ceremony with a military parade and speeches by dignitaries. The total experience made a lasting impression on Coubertin. The mingling of cultures, the celebration of success, and the songs, speeches, and other rituals combined to create an atmosphere that he would try to duplicate in his Olympic Games.

Meanwhile, Coubertin began to tally the results of his survey of physical education programs in French high schools. He found that most of the schools provided few, if any, opportunities for their students to learn and play the sports that he felt would strengthen their bodies and minds. Coubertin had formed a committee to encourage the development of such programs, and it had proposed a "congress on physical exercises" to take place as part of the 1889 Exposition. Students from various high schools competed in gymnastics, rowing, swimming, track, and several other sports. Although the congress received little attention in the midst of the greater excitement of the Exposition, it was an important step for Coubertin. It helped him formulate an idea for a larger sports festival.

In November 1892, Coubertin announced that he planned to revive the Olympic Games by holding a grand international sports competition. He traveled to the United States the following year and shared his vision with officials at universities across the country. When he returned home, Coubertin organized a conference to draw up the rules and format of the Games. A total of 79 official delegates from 12 countries attended the opening banquet on June 16, 1894. Under Coubertin's direction, they voted to hold the Games every four years and to feature only modern, rather than ancient, sports. They also decided to move the Games to a different site each time and to create an International Olympic Committee (IOC). Members of the IOC would be responsible for communicating the principles and purpose of the Olympics to each of their countries.

"Our thought, in reviving an institution which had disappeared for so many centuries, is this," Coubertin wrote. "Athleticism is taking on an importance that grows each year.

On April 6, 1896, approximately 100,000 people gathered in Athens for the opening of the first Modern Olympic Games. Athletes from 14 nations traveled to the Games, with the largest delegations coming from Greece, Germany, and France. Greece would lead all nations with a total of 46 first-, second-, or third-place finishers, but the U.S. would tally more champions. Eleven American athletes finished first in their events, as opposed to ten from Greece.

IN ATHENS, GYMNASTICS EVENTS TOOK PLACE OUTDOORS, IN THE PANATHENAIC STADIUM. HERE, GERMANY'S CARL SCHUHMANN PERFORMS IN THE LONG HORSE VAULT. SCHUHMANN WENT ON TO TAKE FIRST PLACE IN THE EVENT. HE ALSO SHARED ANOTHER FIRST-PLACE FINISH AS PART OF GERMANY'S 10-MAN ROSTER IN THE TEAM HORIZONTAL BAR EVENT.

Its role promises to be as considerable and durable in the modern world as it was in the ancient world; moreover, it reappears with new characteristics: it is international and democratic, as a result, appropriate to the needs and ideas of the present time."

Coubertin originally thought the first modern Olympic Games should take place as part of the 1900 Exposition in Paris, but the delegates at the conference didn't want to wait six years. So Coubertin conferred with the Greek delegate, who agreed that Athens would host the first modern Games in 1896. Under the leadership of Crown Prince Constantine, the Greek Organizing Committee quickly got busy raising funds from private citizens. A wealthy businessman donated the money for the centerpiece of the Games, the Panathenaic Stadium. Hundreds of laborers rebuilt this white marble structure from the ruins of an ancient stadium that dated back to 330 B.C.

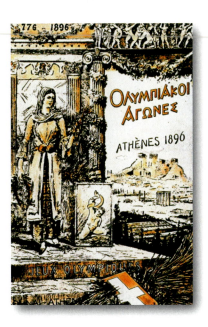

Historians estimate that from 80,000 to 120,000 people witnessed the opening ceremonies of the first modern Olympics, half in the stadium and half looking on from the surrounding hills. They saw the Greek royal family enter the stadium and King George officially proclaim "the opening of the first international Olympic Games at Athens." Most of the 245 men competing in the Games stood in two lines in the center of the arena as pigeons were released and a chorus of 150 people sang the newly written Olympic hymn. "Immortal Spirit of antiquity," they sang, "Give light and vitality to these noble games: throw imperishable floral crowns to the victors in the running, wrestling, and discus, and with thy light animate hearts of steel!"

Competition started immediately, with Francis Lane of the United States winning the first event at the modern Olympics, a heat (preliminary round) in the 100-meter sprint. Americans won the other two heats in the 100, but the final would not take place for four days. Instead, the first Olympic final was in the triple jump, and American James Connolly won the event. Connolly had dropped out of Harvard University after the school refused his request for time off to travel to Athens for the Olympics. He would also finish second in the high jump and third in the long jump.

Over the course of 11 days, athletes from 14 nations competed in a total of 43 events in track and field, gymnastics, swimming, tennis, cycling, wrestling, fencing, shooting, and weight lifting. The rowing and yachting contests were canceled due to bad weather. Winners received silver medals, crowns made of olive branches, and certificates. Second-place finishers received certificates, bronze medals, and crowns made of laurel. (The practice of awarding gold, silver, and bronze medals for first, second, and third place did not begin until 1904.) To the dismay of the host country,

ALTHOUGH THE SYSTEM OF REWARD-ING GOLD, SILVER, AND BRONZE MEDALS DID NOT BEGIN UNTIL 1904, A COMMEMORATIVE COIN WAS ISSUED FOR THE 1896 GAMES (TOP). SO WAS AN OFFICIAL POSTER, SHOWN HERE.

the United States dominated the track and field contests, winning 9 of the first 11 events. That put even more pressure on the Greek runners in the longest event, the marathon.

Today, historians think that the 1896 marathon was the first defining moment for the modern Olympic Games. Before it was run, the Greek audience had begun to lose interest in the Games. No single athlete or event had gotten their hearts pumping the way great sports contests should. After their countrymen failed to win any track and field events, the Greek people began to pray and plead for one of their athletes to win the marathon. The fact that this race was seeped in Greek legend added to its significance. In ancient times, runners often covered long distances to tell of military victories or deliver other news. One particular legend recalled a messenger who ran from the city of Marathon to Athens to announce a victory before he dropped dead of exhaustion. Like that legendary journey, the 1896 marathon would start at Marathon and cover 24 miles, 4,514 feet to the Panathenaic Stadium in Athens.

Although Greece had selected its Olympic marathoners by having them run that distance in trial races, only one of the other competitors had ever run so far. Inexperience took its toll, as several runners set a fast pace and then collapsed. Meanwhile, the Greek runners bided their time. After more than three-quarters of the race, a 24-year-old shepherd named Spiridon Loues caught up with the front-runner and eventually pulled ahead. A messenger on horseback quickly headed off to the stadium to tell the king that a Greek athlete was in the lead.

By the time Loues made his way into the stadium, the crowd of more than 100,000 people was on its feet, cheering wildly. Crown Prince Constantine and

his brother, Prince George, rushed down from the royal box and ran to the finish line with Loues, as fans showered him with flowers and threw their hats in the air. His number, 17, was raised up a flagpole along with the Greek flag, and a flock of white doves was released. Then the princes lifted Loues on their shoulders and carried him in triumph. Forty years later Loues would say, "That hour was something unimaginable and it still appears to me in my memory like a dream."

There have been many more defining moments at the Olympic Games since Spiridon Loues won the marathon that April day in 1896. Thousands of athletes have experienced the thrill of striving to finish "swifter, higher, stronger"— the motto that Pierre de Coubertin adopted for the Olympics from a French priest. Yet if Coubertin had gotten his way, a good number of those Olympians never would have been able to compete. It took a feisty Frenchwoman to force the door open for them.

MOST OF THE ATHLETES ON THE FIRST U.S. WOMEN'S TRACK TEAM TO COMPETE OVERSEAS WERE STILL IN

HIGH SCHOOL. THE TEAM, WHICH TRAVELED TO PARIS FOR THE WOMEN'S OLYMPICS IN 1922, INCLUDED,

LEFT TO RIGHT, ELIZABETH STINE, MABEL GILLILAND, CAMELIA SABIE, FLOREIDA BATSON, JANET SNOW,

AND ESTHER GREEN. TOP, THE WARM-UP JACKET OF ONE OF GREAT BRITAIN'S EARLIEST FEMALE OLYMPIC

TRACK STARS, 1932 BRONZE MEDALIST (IN THE 4 X 100-METER RELAY) GWENDOLINA PORTER

PIERRE DE COUBERTIN NEVER WANTED WOMEN to compete at the Olympic Games. "I feel that the Olympics must be reserved for men," he wrote during the fifth Olympiad in 1912. He scoffed at the idea that female athletes could hold their own against males. "Whatever the athletic ambitions of women may be, women cannot claim to outdo men in running, fencing, equestrian events, etc.,"

WOMEN DIG IN THEIR HEELS

he wrote. Coubertin also rejected the idea that women should have separate events. Holding "a little female Olympiad alongside the great male Olympiad," he concluded, was "impractical, uninteresting, ungainly, and, I do not hesitate to add, improper." Such a women's competition was not in keeping with his vision of the Games as "the solemn and periodic exaltation of male athletics...with the applause of women as a reward."

Coubertin reflected the conservative views of many Frenchmen. They honored women as wives and mothers but disapproved of them entering arenas they considered exclusively male. Yet the increasing popularity of the bicycle in France in the 1890s had started to change some men's views about athletic activity. Cycling became a social event for men and women, and the sport gradually became acceptable for the "fairer sex." So did other social sports such as archery, tennis, ice skating, and golf. Indeed, these were the first sports added for women at the Olympic Games.

Gymnastics, too, was growing in popularity in France as a way to ensure that women would become physically fit. And some gymnastics programs included track and field events. These competitions led to a mounting effort to persuade the IOC to add women's track and field contests to the Olympic Games. But with Pierre de Coubertin still at the helm, the IOC stubbornly refused. Fittingly, an equally stubborn Frenchwoman was behind the campaign to bring about change.

Like Coubertin, Alice Milliat believed in the value of sport in building character and physical strength. She was a translator by profession and had taken up rowing after being widowed at an early age. Milliat helped to found the group that held the first national women's sports championships in France. After the IOC denied all requests to add women's Olympic track and field events, she formed her own worldwide sports organization, the Federation Sportive Feminine Intérnationale (FSFI). Five other countries joined France as the initial members: Czechoslovakia, Great Britain, Italy, Switzerland, and the United States.

Milliat's FSFI had two main goals. The first was to get the International Amateur Athletic Federation (IAAF), which oversaw track and field competitions, to recognize women's events. The second was to persuade the IOC to add women's track and field to the Olympics. To achieve those goals, the FSFI organized its own competition, the Women's Olympic Games. The first Women's Olympics consisted of a one-day track meet held in Paris on April 20, 1922. Close to 20,000 people watched 65 female athletes from five nations take part in 11 events—and break 18 women's world records in the process.

When he learned about Milliat's activities, Coubertin was not pleased. First, he and the IOC demanded that she immediately remove the word "Olympics" from her Games. Then they ordered the IAAF to wrest control of women's track and field from Milliat's group. After two years of negotiations, Milliat agreed to change the name of her festival and adopt the IAAF's rules if the IAAF would recommend that the IOC add women's track events to the 1928 Olympics. It was the beginning of a power struggle that would last more than a decade.

In 1926, the FSFI held its second sports festival, renamed the Women's World Games. Women from eight countries traveled to Göteborg, Sweden, to compete in 15 track and field events at the three-day meet. Meanwhile, Pierre de Coubertin had ended

After running her own successful women's sports competitions in 1922 and 1926, Alice Milliat helped persuade the IOC to add women's track events to the Olympics. Below, a heat in the 60-meter hurdles at the 1922 Women's Olympics. Above, Milliat, left, poses with an international group of track officials at the 1928 Olympics.

NEWSPAPER REPORTS OF THE 1928 WOMEN'S OLYMPIC 800-METER RACE, SHOWN HERE, GREATLY EXAGGERATED THE LEVEL OF EXHAUSTION OF SOME OF THE FINISHERS. THE NEW IOC PRESIDENT, HENRI DE BAILLET-LATOUR, WAS SO CONCERNED THAT HE SUGGESTED CUTTING ALL WOMEN'S EVENTS IN ALL SPORTS FROM FUTURE OLYMPIADS.

a 29-year run as president of the IOC in 1925. Against his advice, the IOC agreed to include five women's track and field events at the 1928 Olympics on a trial basis.

As it turned out, women set or equaled women's world records in four of the five track and field events at the 1928 Olympics. But exaggerated reports of what happened at the end of the 800-meter race nearly destroyed any progress women had made. The 800, a distance of about half a mile, featured one runner who was recovering from a leg injury and several others who usually ran sprints. When a few of the athletes dropped to the ground after finishing the race, their detractors had a field day. "The final of the women's 800-meter run...plainly demonstrated that even this distance makes too great a call on feminine strength," wrote Wythe Williams of the *New York Times*.

In 1929, the IOC voted to eliminate women's track and field events from the Olympics, but it reversed the ruling under pressure from the United States. Still, only one more women's track and field event was added to the lineup at the 1932 Olympics. Meanwhile, Alice Milliat continued with her Women's World Games. In 1930, more than 200 athletes from 17 countries gathered for a three-day meet in Prague, Czechoslovakia. Four years later, the FSFI held its fourth, and final, Women's World Games when athletes from 19 countries met in London.

By that time, Alice Milliat realized that the IOC had no interest in expanding the women's program at the Olympics. So she wrote the IOC a letter asking that all women's events be cut. Her idea was to hold a true, separate Women's Olympics with a whole range of sports. But the IOC never voted on Milliat's proposal. Instead, the IAAF took control of women's track and field. The group accepted all records set at FSFI competitions and recommended a complete slate of women's events at the Olympics. Milliat had won the fight, but her organization no longer had a purpose. After 15 years of agitating for women's sports, the FSFI—and Alice Milliat—disappeared from the scene.

Today, historians give Milliat credit for speeding up the expansion of the women's program at the Olympics. The outspoken Milliat knew the benefits of sport for women because she had enjoyed them herself. Her beliefs and experiences made her a determined crusader against Pierre de Coubertin and his male cronies. "The men involved in men's sports do not realize that they could do themselves a favor by showing some interest in women's sport," Milliat said in 1927. "[Instead,] they shut themselves away in their everlasting male egoism."

GISELA MAUERMEYER OF GERMANY PUT THE SHOT 44 FEET, 10 INCHES TO WIN THE EVENT AT THE 1934 WOMEN'S WORLD GAMES. ALTHOUGH THE WOMEN'S SHOT PUT WAS NOT ADDED TO THE OLYMPICS UNTIL 1948, MAUERMEYER WOULD WIN OLYMPIC GOLD IN THE DISCUS THROW IN 1936.

Jesse Owens (right) broke the Olympic record for the 200-meter sprint in this heat at the 1936 Summer Games. Then he broke it again in the final. The silver medalist in the event was Matthew "Mack" Robinson, whose younger brother Jackie would later become the first African American to play major league baseball in the 20th century. Top, a shoe worn by Owens in his long jump victory, designed by Adi Dassler, founder of Adidas

LTHOUGH POWER STRUGGLES AND POLITICS have always played a part at the Olympics, it is the awe-inspiring athletic performances that have made the Games the grandest sports spectacle in the world. Those who compete at the Olympic Games are members of an elite class of athletes who take the field on behalf of their countries as well as themselves. Among them, there have been a handful of

BREAKTHROUGH
ATHLETES

breakthrough stars who have raised the level of the Games thanks to a combination of amazing talent, unwavering dedication, and dynamic personal appeal. The history of the Summer Olympics can be told through their accomplishments.

During the early years of the modern Olympics, Jim Thorpe set the standard for excellence. Thorpe was a Native American athlete who had excelled in football, baseball, track and field, and several other sports at the Carlisle Indian School in Pennsylvania. At the Stockholm Games in 1912, he astonished spectators by winning both the five-event pentathlon and the ten-event decathlon. (He also came in fourth in the high jump and seventh in the long jump.) When King Gustav V of Sweden presented him with his medals, he told Thorpe, "Sir, you are the greatest

athlete in the world." Thorpe remains the only athlete to win the pentathlon and the decathlon at the same Olympics.

After he returned to the United States, Thorpe received a letter from President William Howard Taft congratulating him on his "magnificent victories." Yet his triumphs would be short-lived. In 1913, Thorpe admitted that he had earned $15 per week playing two seasons of semipro baseball, a violation of the complicated Olympic rules on amateurism. The IOC had no choice but to strip him of his medals. Thorpe went on to play professional baseball and football and to act in more than 20 Hollywood films. In 1950, the Associated Press voted him the greatest male athlete of the first half of the 20th century. Although Thorpe died in 1953, his family doggedly fought to have his Olympic achievements reinstated. In 1982, the IOC finally agreed, recasting his gold medals and presenting them to Thorpe's seven children.

Following World War I, another track star came to dominate the Olympics. Paavo Nurmi was the first of the "Flying Finns," runners from Finland known for their speed and endurance. At the 1920 Olympics, Nurmi won three gold medals—in the 10,000-meter race, the 8,000-meter cross-country race, and a team cross-country event. He also took the silver medal in the 5,000-meter race. But it was his performance at the 1924 Olympics that elevated him to superstar status. Nurmi won the gold medal in the 1,500 meters, a distance of about one mile. Then, only one hour later, he won the gold in the 5,000 meters. It was a feat, Olympic historian Bud Greenspan said in 1996, "that today still stands as the greatest individual track and field performance in history."

Nurmi won three more gold medals in 1924, and one gold and two silvers at the 1928 Games. His total of nine gold and three silver medals places him among the top Olympic medal winners of all time. Yet he might have added to it. Nurmi was in training to run the marathon at the 1932 Olympics, but like Thorpe, he was tripped up by the Olympic rules on amateurism. Officials charged that he had accepted money above and beyond his expenses during an exhibition tour, and he was barred from the 1932

PAAVO NURMI PLANNED HIS RACES IN ADVANCE, AND FREQUENTLY CHECKED HIS STOPWATCH TO MAKE SURE HE REACHED HIS CHECKPOINTS EXACTLY ON TIME. HE WAS CONFIDENT THAT HIS EXCELLENT CONDITIONING WOULD CARRY HIM PAST ALL COMPETITORS IN THE CLOSING MOMENTS OF ANY RACE.

BABE DIDRIKSON LATER DESCRIBED HER FIRST OLYMPIC JAVELIN THROW AS AWKWARD. "IT WAS," SHE SAID,

"LIKE A CATCHER'S PEG FROM HOME PLATE TO SECOND BASE" INSTEAD OF AN ELEGANT ARCHING MISSILE.

THE TOSS WENT 143 FEET, 4 INCHES AND SET AN OLYMPIC RECORD, BUT IT ALSO TORE CARTILAGE IN HER

RIGHT SHOULDER. DIDRIKSON KEPT THE INJURY QUIET SO AS NOT TO GIVE HER OPPONENTS AN ADVANTAGE.

Games. Nurmi had the chance to return to glory in 1952, when he carried the Olympic torch into the stadium at the start of the Helsinki Games. After he died in 1973, he received a state funeral attended by President Urho Kekkonen of Finland, a former teammate at the 1924 Olympics.

When Mildred "Babe" Didrikson took the Olympic stage in 1932, she sent sportswriters searching for adjectives and competitors running for cover. Didrikson was brash, bold, and cocky, a new phenomenon among female athletes. She had single-handedly won the track meet that served as the Olympic trials by earning gold medals in six of the ten events and scoring more points on her own than every whole team that entered. At the Los Angeles Games, she was limited by a rule that allowed women to compete in only three track and field events. She won gold medals in the javelin and 80-meter hurdles, and tied for first place in the high jump with teammate Jean Shiley. Officials gave Shiley the gold and Didrikson the silver because they determined that Babe's headfirst style over the bar was illegal. Despite this fact, both athletes got credit for setting the new world record.

Like Thorpe and Nurmi, Didrikson's Olympic career was cut short when she was accused of forfeiting her amateur status. In Didrikson's case, a 1933 ad for a Dodge automobile used a photo showing her jumping over a hurdle and stated, "Dodge 6....The stuff that makes real champions—Babe Didrikson." Didrikson claimed she had nothing to do with the ad and hadn't received any money for it, and the auto dealer backed her up. But she was barred from future Olympiads. She went on to compete in a whole host of other sports, finally settling on golf. Didrikson was one of the founding members of the Ladies Professional Golf Association and thrilled crowds with her hard-hitting style. Before dying of cancer in 1956, she was voted the greatest female athlete of the first half of the 20th century by the Associated Press.

Because of the dominance of track and field events at the early Olympic Games, the most influential athletes often came from that sport. In 1936 track star Jesse Owens (*see page 28*) turned in a performance that echoed beyond the playing field into the realm of politics and world affairs. Owens was one of many African-American athletes competing at the 11th Olympiad in Nazi Germany. Under the policies of German Chancellor Adolf Hitler, the white, Aryan race ruled supreme, and blacks and Jews were openly tormented. Although Hitler scaled back his racist policies during the Olympics, the atmosphere was still tense. But the German crowds were awed by Owens as he won gold medals in the 100-meter sprint, the 200-meter sprint, the long jump, and the 4 x 100-meter relay. He was mobbed by fans seeking autographs the entire time he was in Germany.

Owens excelled on the field and conducted himself with dignity in the face of extreme prejudice. Back in the United States, though, he had to contend with more subtle forms of discrimination. "I came back to my native country, and I could not ride in the front of the bus," he said. "I had to go to the back door. I couldn't live where I wanted." To make ends meet, Owens entered into a number of different business ventures and for a time used his athletic skills to race against horses, dogs, and motorcycle riders. But he found his greatest success as a professional speaker, sharing his insights about sports and life. Owens became an enduring role model for Americans

of all backgrounds, receiving the Presidential Medal of Freedom from President Gerald Ford in 1976. Four years after Owens died, his granddaughter, Gina Hemphill, honored his memory by carrying the torch into Los Angeles Coliseum to kick off the 1984 Olympics.

At the 1948 Summer Olympics, Fanny Blankers-Koen of the Netherlands caused a lot of people to reexamine their thoughts on sports and motherhood. As a teenager in 1936, Blankers-Koen had failed to win a medal at the Berlin Games. She continued to train during World War II, and by the time the London Games came around in 1948, she held six world records in running and jumping events. But she was also the mother of two children, and many people objected to her competing. "Why is a 30-year-old mother of two running in short pants at the expense of leaving her family?" one British Olympic official asked.

Blankers-Koen responded by boldly entering four events, the maximum allowed for women. She won gold medals in the 100-meter sprint, the 200-meter sprint, the 80-meter hurdles, and as the anchor, or final runner, of the Dutch 4 x 100-meter relay team. Blankers-Koen was the first female athlete to win four gold medals in track and field at a single Olympics, and through 2004 was still the only one to do so. But her favorite Olympic memory had nothing to do with her own medals. It involved her idol Jesse Owens, whose autograph she had received at the 1936 Games. "When I met him again in Munich at the 1972 Olympics I said, 'I still have your autograph, I'm Fanny Blankers-Koen,'" she told a British newspaper in 2002. "He said, 'You don't have to tell me who you are, I know everything about you.' Isn't that incredible? Jesse Owens knew who I was."

While Blankers-Koen made people rethink their opinions of athletes who were mothers, Wilma Rudolph helped improve the image of all women in

WILMA RUDOLPH DEVELOPED HER MAJESTIC RUNNING STYLE AT TENNESSEE STATE UNIVERSITY, ONE OF THE HISTORICALLY BLACK COLLEGES THAT WERE AT THE FOREFRONT OF WOMEN'S TRACK AND FIELD. HER COACH, ED TEMPLE, SERVED AS COACH OF THE U.S. WOMEN'S OLYMPIC TRACK TEAM IN 1960 AND 1964. HERE, RUDOLPH CROSSES THE FINISH LINE AS ANCHOR OF THE 4 X 100-METER RELAY TEAM AT THE 1960 GAMES.

track and field. In 1960, many people still agreed with IOC president Avery Brundage, who once said, "I am fed up to the ears with women as track and field competitors. Their charms sink to less than zero." Brundage and others felt that the sport caused women to develop muscles and raw strength at the expense of their femininity. Then came Rudolph, a 5-foot, 11-inch sprinter whose fluid style earned her the nickname "The Black Gazelle" from the European press. "Wilma's accomplishments opened up the door for women in track because of her grace and beauty," said Nell Jackson, who coached her on the 1956 Olympic track team. "People saw her as beauty in motion."

A worldwide TV audience watched Rudolph win three gold medals at the 1960 Olympics in the 100-meter sprint, the 200-meter sprint, and the 4 x 100-meter relay. Soon afterward, high schools and colleges in the U.S. started making a determined effort to train more girls in track and field. Rudolph did her part, too, after she retired from competition in 1962. She coached track at DePauw University in Indiana and started the Wilma Rudolph Foundation to support sports programs for kids. Rudolph, who wore braces on her legs and was partially paralyzed from age 4 to 11, taught kids to have winning attitudes as well as winning moves. "I remind them [that] the triumph can't be had without the struggle," she once told ESPN. Rudolph died of brain cancer in 1994.

TV audiences saw Wilma Rudolph run via black-and-white videotape, but by 1972 the Olympic Games were broadcast live and in color. It's appropriate, then, that the standout athlete of those games happened to have matinee-idol good looks to go along with his record-breaking performance. Mark Spitz was a California-born swimmer who'd had a disappointing Olympics in 1968, winning two gold medals in team relays, but only a silver and a bronze in individual events. After that he entered Indiana University to train with former Olympic team coach James "Doc" Counsilman. Spitz started consistently winning medals and awards in college competitions, and he peaked at the Munich Games. He won individual gold medals in the 100-meter butterfly, the 200-meter butterfly, the 100-meter freestyle, and the 200-meter freestyle, all in world-record time. He also led the U.S. to three gold medals in the relays, with the team setting a world record in each race.

Spitz is the only athlete to win seven gold medals at a single Olympiad. Through the 2004 Summer Games, he was one of only four Olympians to win a total of nine gold medals. Soon after the 1972 Games, a poster showing Spitz wearing a swimsuit and his seven gold medals from Munich became a bestseller. Spitz was one of the first Olympians to retire and take advantage of the commercial rewards that came his way, earning more than $5 million from his endorsement contracts. He also worked in broadcasting and guest starred on several TV programs before starting a real estate business in Los Angeles. Though Spitz mounted a comeback in the early 1990s, he couldn't compete with the younger generation of swimmers. Today he still swims, more slowly, just for fun.

Also in the 1970s, two teenagers won the hearts of audiences and caused a huge surge in popularity for the sport of gymnastics. Olga Korbut was 17 years old when her spectacular routine on the uneven bars helped win the team competition at the Munich Olympic Games for the Soviet Union. (From 1922–1991, the Soviet Union,

Mark Spitz sets a new world record in the men's 200-meter butterfly at the Olympic swimming trials in August 1972 (above), and a month later shows off five of the seven gold medals he would win at the 1972 Summer Games. He set a new world record in each of his 1972 Olympic medal–winning efforts.

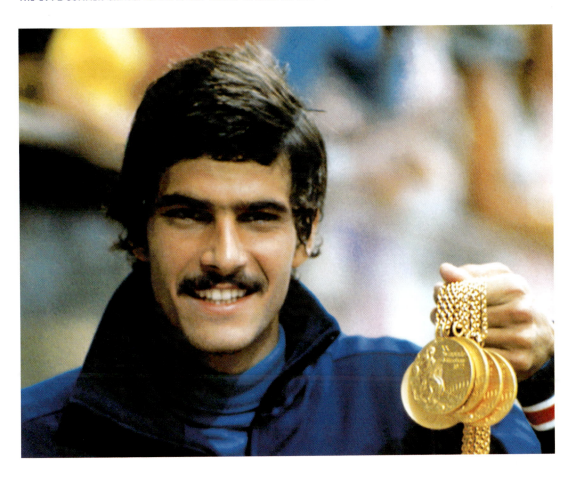

or U.S.S.R., was a country made up of 15 republics including Russia.) Korbut also won gold medals in the balance beam and the floor exercises, as well as a silver medal in the individual uneven bars. She returned to lead the Soviets to a team gold medal at the 1976 Olympics, but this time there was another teen sensation to contend with. Fourteen-year-old Nadia Comaneci of Romania earned a perfect 10 on the uneven bars, the first such score in the history of Olympic gymnastics. During her time in Montreal Comaneci went on to score six more perfect 10s and win three gold medals, for the individual all-around competition, the balance beam, and the uneven bars. In addition, she shared a silver medal for the team competition and won bronze in the floor exercises.

With the successes of Korbut and Comaneci, women's gymnastics became a sport dominated by agile, young athletes doing bold jumps and maneuvering their bodies into almost impossible positions. The effects were stunning and dramatic, but the teenagers who followed Korbut and Comaneci into the sport faced unexpected challenges. Some gymnasts hid injuries to keep practicing and remain competitive, doing permanent damage to their bodies. Others, including Comaneci herself, developed eating disorders as a result of efforts to keep their weight down and their bodies small. Eventually, officials passed a rule that all gymnasts must be at least 16 during the calendar year of an Olympics in order to compete. With this age requirement officials aimed to help Olympic gymnasts deal with the stresses of competing as well as with their victories. Both Korbut and Comaneci had trouble adjusting to everyday life after experiencing the glare of the international spotlight at a young age.

For Greg Louganis, the sport of diving provided a refuge from stress and a chance to make sense of the rest of his life. Louganis is considered by many to be the best male diver ever to compete at the Olympics. He scored a rare double in 1984 by winning gold medals in both springboard and platform diving, with point totals that were significantly higher than those of any other diver in history. Four years later, Louganis went to Seoul, South Korea, to defend his titles. He looked certain to do so, until he smacked his head on the end of the springboard during the qualifying round. Remarkably, he returned 35 minutes later to nail the last qualifying dive. Louganis went on to win the springboard and platform titles again, joining 1950s women's champion Pat McCormick as the only divers to score back-to-back doubles in diving.

GREG LOUGANIS SHOWS PERFECT FORM AS HE COMPETES AT THE U.S. NATIONAL DIVING CHAMPIONSHIPS BEFORE THE 1988 SUMMER OLYMPICS (ABOVE). IN SEOUL, HOWEVER, HE HORRIFIES SPECTATORS WHEN HE HITS HIS HEAD ON THE SPRINGBOARD DURING THE QUALIFYING ROUND.

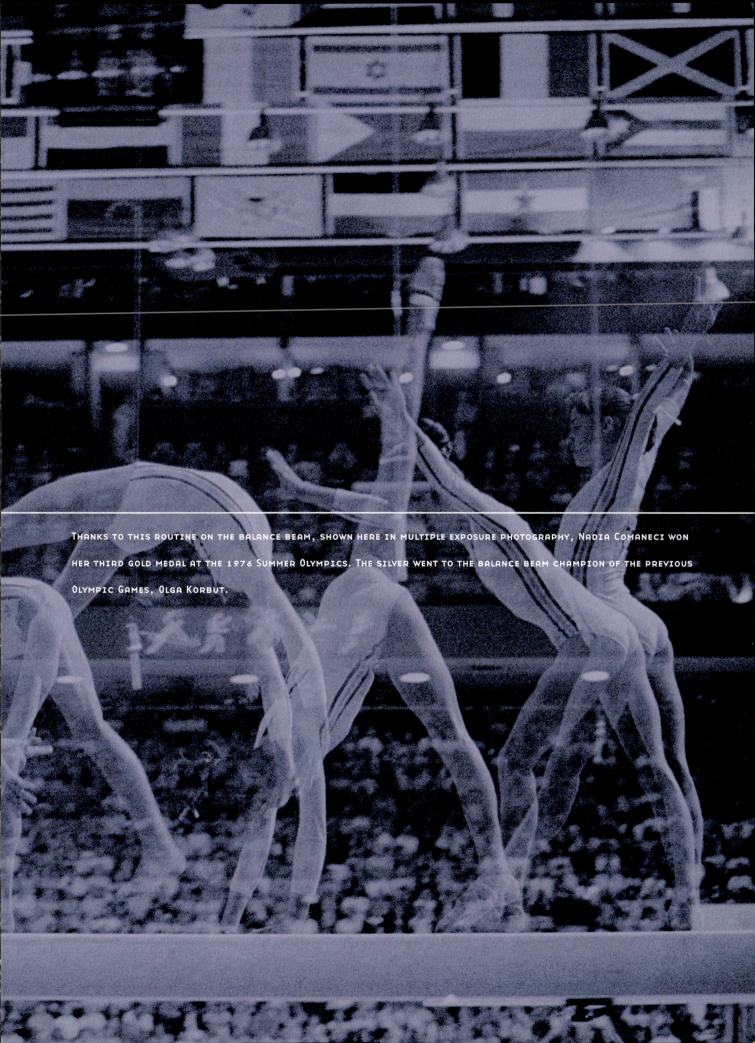

Thanks to this routine on the balance beam, shown here in multiple exposure photography, Nadia Comaneci won her third gold medal at the 1976 Summer Olympics. The silver went to the balance beam champion of the previous Olympic Games, Olga Korbut.

Born in 1962, Jackie Joyner-Kersee was named after Jacqueline Kennedy, wife of then-President John F. Kennedy. Her grandmother explained why. "Someday," she said, "this girl will be the first lady of something." As she closed out her career, sportswriters agreed that she was indeed the "first lady of track and field." Above, she shows her form in the long jump, and below competes in her last heptathlon at the 1996 Olympics.

These accomplishments are even more impressive considering that Louganis survived a rocky childhood. He was born in San Diego, California, to teenage parents of Samoan and European backgrounds who gave him up for adoption. Kids made fun of his dark skin and of the difficulties he had in school because he suffered from dyslexia. As a teenager, he also came to realize he was gay, a secret that he kept from others. He started experimenting with drugs and alcohol at an early age. But Louganis also started fooling around on the diving board at his family's pool, using the gymnastics and dance moves he'd learned in classes after school. "Diving was my salvation," he would later say. He retired from the sport following the 1988 Games and began working as an actor. Louganis disclosed that he was suffering from AIDS after writing his autobiography in 1995. His health stabilized with medication, he became active in groups that educate young people about dyslexia, drug and alcohol abuse, and AIDS prevention.

As the 20th century drew to a close, the number of women's events at the Olympics increased and the achievements of female athletes came to the fore. Looking ahead to the Atlanta Games, *Newsweek* magazine labeled 1996 the "Year of the Women," predicting that "this summer's Centennial Olympic Games fairly promise to be dominated by women athletes." Those Games saw women win 19 of the 44 U.S. gold medals, including team medals in soccer, softball, basketball, and gymnastics. But they also featured the swan song of a woman who had helped usher in the new era of female empowerment, track and field star Jackie Joyner-Kersee. After winning back-to-back gold medals in the heptathlon in 1988 and 1992, Joyner-Kersee had to withdraw from that event in 1996 due to a hamstring injury. But she gamely competed in the long jump, pulling out a bronze medal with one last dazzling jump. Her total Olympic haul, from 1984 through 1996, was three gold medals, one silver, and two bronze.

Called "the best woman athlete ever" by *Newsweek,* Joyner-Kersee rewrote the record books on the heptathlon. This event, the most grueling one in the women's program, combines the shot put, javelin, 100-meter hurdles, 200-meter sprint, 800-meter run, high jump, and long jump. Joyner-Kersee set a heptathlon world record in 1988, scoring 7,291 points. When she officially retired in 2001, she still held the record, as well as the next five highest scores. Since then she has dedicated herself to providing kids with opportunities to excel in both sports and academics. Toward that end, she opened the Jackie Joyner-Kersee Boys & Girls Club in her hometown of East St. Louis, Illinois. The club stands on the site of the recreation center where she played and practiced as a girl.

Before he changed his name and became the world heavyweight boxing champion, ★ MUHAMMAD ALI ★ boxed at the Olympics. In 1960, Ali competed in Rome under his birth name of Cassius Clay and took the gold medal in the light heavyweight division. The 18-year-old from Louisville, Kentucky, would turn pro later that year and win the first of his three world heavyweight crowns in 1964.

★ ABEBE BIKILA ★ of Ethiopia was the first black African to win the Olympic marathon and the first athlete to win two marathons in a row. Bikila ran the 26 miles, 385 yards barefoot in 1960 because his new running shoes pinched his feet. In 1964 he wore running shoes and finished in 2 hours, 12 minutes, 11.2 seconds, three minutes faster than his shoeless effort.

Jumping champ ★ RAY EWRY ★ is unofficially number one in total Olympic gold medals won. The Indiana native won three at the 1900 Games, three in 1904, and two in 1908, as well as two at the 1906 Interim Games. Those Interim Games were held to work out the kinks in the Olympic format, and don't count as an official Olympiad. So Ewry's two 1906 medals don't formally count.

Not even surgery could keep ★ JOAN BENOIT ★ from running the first Olympic women's marathon. Benoit had surgery on her right knee only 17 days before the Olympic trials, but she recovered quickly. After winning the trials, she scored a decisive victory at the 1984 Games by breaking away from the pack after 14 minutes and leading the rest of the way. She finished in 2 hours, 24 minutes, 52 seconds, looking fit and in command.

★ **NAWAL EL MOUTAWAKEL** ★ became the first woman from an Islamic country to win an Olympic medal when she took the gold in the 400-meter hurdles at the 1984 Summer Games. She was also the first athlete from Morocco, male or female, ever to win a gold medal. In 1998, El Moutawakel became the first Muslim woman ever elected to the IOC.

2004 Olympic Basketball Ticket

From 1984 through 2000, there was one constant on the U.S. women's Olympic basketball team, ★ **TERESA EDWARDS.** ★ The most decorated basketball player in Olympic history, this University of Georgia grad helped lead the U.S. to four gold medals and one bronze. "My joy in life is playing basketball," Edwards said after winning her fifth Olympic medal.

EXCELLING

★ **EMIL ZÁTOPEK** ★ of Czechoslovakia started the 1952 Olympics by winning both the 10,000-meter race and the 5,000-meter race. After watching his wife, Dana Zátopková, win the gold medal in the javelin, he decided he was ready for one more challenge. Although he had never run a marathon before, he entered and won by two and a half minutes. Zátopek is the only person to win the 5,000, the 10,000, and the marathon in a single Olympiad.

★ **CARL LEWIS** ★ began his Olympic career in 1984 by repeating Jesse Owens's sweep of the 100-meter and 200-meter sprints, the long jump, and the 4 x 100-meter relay. But he was just getting started. Lewis won the long jump again in 1988, 1992, and 1996, and added two more gold medals and a silver as well. He is one of only four Olympians to win nine gold medals, and one of only three to win the same individual event four times.

At the 1968 Olympics, U.S. track stars Tommie Smith (center) and John Carlos (right) used the medal ceremony for the 200-meter sprint to record a silent protest against racism by giving the Black Power salute. Olympic officials were so angry that they threatened to disqualify the entire U.S. track-and-field team if Smith and Carlos were not sent home immediately. Top, a 1968 gold medal

ALTHOUGH THE **O**LYMPIC **G**AMES often bring out the best in the world's athletes, they also have given rise to a whole host of controversies. Issues from conflicts over amateur status to gender testing, from drug use to political boycotts and confrontations have cast a shadow over the Games as a joyous celebration of athletic achievement. The opportunities for scandal and wrongdoing have

CONTROVERSIES
CAST A SHADOW

increased as the Games have grown to massive proportions. It was inevitable that these negative influences, too, would shape the history of the Summer Olympics.

Pierre de Coubertin anticipated problems involving athletes' amateur status at the very first meeting of the IOC in 1894. While Coubertin worked out the format of the Olympic Games, another committee wrote the rules on who was eligible to compete. Members of that committee saw sports as a way to develop character. They wanted to ensure that athletes took part in the Olympics for the experience of competing, rather than for financial gain. They decided that coaches and gymnastics instructors who were paid salaries could not be Olympic athletes, nor could

For Andre Agassi, shown with his 1996 tennis singles gold medal, competing in the Olympics was a family tradition. His father, Mike, represented his native Iran as a boxer at both the 1948 and 1952 Summer Games. Mike lost in the first round both times.

anyone who had accepted prize money for winning any sporting event, ever. But athletes who accepted money to cover their expenses while they trained for the Olympics were eligible.

Over the years, the rules on amateurism were tested many times. Some athletes, including Jim Thorpe and Babe Didrikson, were severely punished for minor infractions while others who committed more serious violations were never discovered. Then, in the 1950s, athletes from communist countries began to dominate certain sports. Those athletes trained full time and had all of their expenses paid by their governments, but still were considered amateurs. Some observers grew increasingly frustrated with the blurring distinction between amateur and professional athletes. They argued that the Olympics should be open to any athlete who competed in sport for the pursuit of excellence, whether or not that person was an amateur.

Eventually, the IOC reconsidered its policy on amateurism. In 1986, it revised the Olympic charter to allow the international federation that controls each sport to decide which athletes are eligible to compete. That resulted in some tricky formulas. For example, FIFA, the international federation for soccer, ruled that female players over age 16 and male players under age 23 are eligible for the Olympics, whether they are amateurs or professionals. But each Olympic men's team can add three players 23 or older as exceptions. Baseball allows minor leaguers but not major leaguers, and tennis allows male athletes over age 13 and female athletes over age 14. Despite the prize money available to professional athletes in their regular leagues and tournaments, the Olympics seem to have an unequaled appeal. "To win a Grand Slam is the biggest thing you can accomplish inside your sport," said 1996 tennis gold medalist Andre Agassi, "but the Olympics is the biggest thing you can do in all [of] sports."

At the same time that the controversy over amateurism was heating up, Olympic officials also began debating the issue of gender testing. In 1957, a German high jumper named Hermann Ratjen revealed that Nazi officials had forced him to disguise his gender and compete as a woman at the 1936 Berlin Games. "Dora" Ratjen didn't win a medal; "she" came in fourth. But Ratjen's success in fooling officials alarmed IOC members. They worried that other male impostors might follow Ratjen's example and try to enter women's events. In 1968, they introduced a gender test that aimed to prove that all female competitors truly were female. Male athletes were not tested to prove that they were indeed male.

Gender tests were embarrassing to women. The earliest test, used at international competitions before the 1968 Olympics, required women to undress in front of a panel of doctors who examined them to make sure they had the right female parts. By the 1968 Games, that test had been replaced by one in which a doctor scraped some tissue from inside each female athlete's cheek. This sample was then analyzed

MAJOR LEAGUE BASEBALL'S REFUSAL TO ALLOW ITS TOP STARS TO PLAY AT THE OLYMPICS WAS CITED AS ONE REASON THE SPORT WILL BE DROPPED FROM THE 2012 GAMES. IN 2000, A U.S. TEAM MADE UP OF PAST AND FUTURE MAJOR LEAGUERS BEAT CUBA FOR THE GOLD. HERE, KOREAN PITCHER KOO DAE-SUNG, LEFT, AND CATCHER HONG SUNG-HEON CELEBRATE THEIR BRONZE MEDAL VICTORY THAT YEAR.

to make sure it had two X sex chromosomes, instead of an X and a Y. Sex chromosomes are the part of a human cell that determines whether a person is male or female. Having two X sex chromosomes usually makes a person female; having an X and a Y usually makes a person male.

What the IOC didn't take into account was that science isn't perfect. Medical research shows that some people are born with an X and a Y sex chromosome, but the chemical makeup of their bodies causes them to develop as females. While these people live their entire lives as women, they would fail the gender test given at the Olympics. About one of every 400 female Olympic athletes did fail that test, although many were allowed to compete after passing a second test. Beyond questions of the fairness of the test, though, women athletes protested the very idea that they had to prove their "femaleness." The protesters claimed that gender testing reflected the IOC's general discomfort with muscular women. Said Olympic pentathlete Jane Frederick, "I think they are saying, 'You are so good, we can't believe you're a woman. So prove it.'"

In the 1990s, the movement to discontinue gender testing grew. Dr. James Puffer, chief medical officer of the 1968 U.S. Olympic team, was among those who believed the practice had outlived its purpose of exposing male impostors. For one thing, the drug tests given to the first four finishers in each event, plus two others chosen at random, required an official to watch as an athlete urinated. "So from a practical standpoint," Puffer said in 1996, "it would seem that gender tests are totally unnecessary." The IOC finally agreed. In 1999, it suspended the practice of gender testing all female athletes, starting with the 2000 Games in Sydney. However, Olympic officials reserved the right to conduct tests on individual athletes as needed.

Along with gender testing, the 1968 Olympics also saw the beginning of the IOC's anti-doping program, aimed at detecting any drugs that athletes may have taken to improve their performances. Although one of the underlying purposes of this program was to catch cheaters and ensure a level playing field for all competitors, IOC officials also were concerned with protecting the health of athletes. Performance-enhancing drugs have side effects that can cause irreparable damage. The athletes who competed for East Germany from the 1960s through the 1980s are living examples of that.

East Germany came into being after World War II, when Germany was occupied by the United States, Great Britain, France, and the Soviet Union. The Soviet Union installed a communist government in the east while the other three countries helped to shape a democratic government in West Germany. Like the Soviets, the East Germans developed a state-run sports program that identified promising

WHEN MIA HAMM LED THE U.S. TEAM TO THE FIRST EVER OLYMPIC GOLD MEDAL IN WOMEN'S SOCCER IN 1996, SHE AND ALL FEMALE ATHLETES HAD TO VERIFY THAT THEY WERE INDEED FEMALE. BY THE TIME HAMM RETURNED WITH THE U.S. TEAM IN 2000, GENDER TESTS HAD BEEN DISCONTINUED. HERE, HAMM BATTLES NORWAY'S GOERIL KRINGEN IN THE 2000 FINAL. NORWAY WON, 3-2.

athletes early and spared no expense in training them. As part of their training, the athletes were given handfuls of "vitamins" to take every day.

Years later, East Germany's athletes learned that the "vitamins" actually were anabolic steroids, compounds produced from the male hormone testosterone that increases a person's muscle mass and strength. The pills worked. In the 1970s and 1980s, East Germany won a total of 160 Olympic gold medals, 40 of them in 1976 alone. During that time, East German athletes never failed the drug tests given by the IOC. Still, after U.S. swimmer Shirley Babashoff finished second to East Germans four times, she charged them with taking steroids. This was evident, she said, from the women's large muscles, deep voices, and extraordinarily fast times.

EAST GERMAN WOMEN CELEBRATE THEIR VICTORY IN THE 1976 OLYMPIC 4 X 100-METER MEDLEY RELAY. THEY SET A WORLD RECORD, BEATING THE SECOND-PLACE U.S. TEAM BY CLOSE TO SEVEN SECONDS. LATER, IT WAS REVEALED THAT THE EAST GERMAN WOMEN HAD BEEN GIVEN "VITAMINS," WHICH WERE REALLY STEROIDS.

Babashoff was ridiculed in the press as a sore loser. But when East and West Germany were united in 1989, records were made public showing that an estimated 10,000 athletes had been given drugs on a regular basis.

Today, approximately 1,000 of those athletes face serious health problems. Some women have had miscarriages; some have had children born with birth defects. Some men have grown enlarged breasts. Both males and females have developed twisted spines, failing livers, and numb limbs. "It's terrifying what they did to us," swimmer Carola Beraktschjan told a reporter in 2000. "I took up to 30 pills a day....There was no question you would not take them." One female shot-putter experienced so many changes in her body that she had a sex change operation. "I didn't know who I was," the athlete said. "I wasn't able to identify with my body anymore."

Although East Germany's records serve as proof of its steroid program, most Olympic drug use is harder to document. Testing has revealed some violators.

In 1988, Canada's Ben Johnson was stripped of his gold medal in the 100-meter sprint after he tested positive for anabolic steroids. And U.S. shot-putter C. J. Hunter withdrew from the 2000 Summer Games after his fourth failed drug test. Still, new classes of performance-enhancing drugs are always being developed, and it takes time to come up with tests to detect them.

Even with the most up-to-date tests, there are larger challenges that must be met before drug use will stop. The rewards of winning medals, from applause to million-dollar endorsement contracts, are enough to push some athletes to seek an extra edge from drugs. "Sport must take a long, hard look at itself, and come to terms with the contradictions and tensions that exist within it," wrote Jim Parry, a British professor who has studied the use of drugs by athletes. Parry added that as long as the public hungers for faster times and new world records, Olympians will have to fight the urge to win at any cost. Years ago, Pierre de Coubertin wrote, "The important thing in the Olympic Games is not winning but taking part." The extent to which athletes are using performance-enhancing drugs is an indication of how much times have changed.

Coubertin had several goals in mind when he revived the Olympic Games, and one of his chief motivations was a desire for world peace. During the ancient Olympics, all warring cities or tribes honored a truce that began as early as two months before the Games and ended a month or two after them, to ensure that athletes and spectators could travel safely. Today, the Olympic Charter still embraces peace as one of its fundamental principles. "The goal of the Olympic Movement," it says, "is to contribute to building a peaceful and better world."

SHOT-PUTTER C.J. HUNTER COMPETES AT THE 2000 OLYMPIC TRIALS. HUNTER, WHO AT THE TIME WAS MARRIED TO U.S. TRACK STAR MARION JONES, WITHDREW FROM THE SYDNEY GAMES AFTER FAILING FOUR DRUG TESTS. JONES LATER WOULD ADMIT THAT SHE HAD TAKEN STEROIDS, TOO, AND WOULD FORFEIT THE FIVE MEDALS SHE WON IN SYDNEY.

IN 1936, GERMANY'S DICTATOR, ADOLF HITLER, WAS A FREQUENT SPECTATOR AT BOTH THE WINTER OLYMPICS, HELD IN GARMISCH-PARTENKIRCHEN, GERMANY, AND THE SUMMER OLYMPICS, HELD IN BERLIN. HERE, HE WATCHES THE SUMMER GAMES FROM HIS BOX AT THE OLYMPIC STADIUM WITH UMBERTO, CROWN PRINCE OF ITALY (LEFT).

Even so, politics and wars have infringed upon the modern Olympic Games many times. The Games were canceled in 1916 due to World War I, and in 1940 and 1944 due to World War II. Tensions also ran high between the wars, when Germany was set to host both the Winter and Summer Games in 1936. The country's blatant discrimination against Jews, blacks, and other minorities caused groups around the world to call for a boycott. But Germany agreed to add a Jewish athlete to its team, and the IOC stood by its choice of host country. The only IOC member who continued to speak out against German policies was replaced. In the end, there were no national boycotts against the 1936 Games, though individual athletes did choose to stay home.

Two boycotts did take place during the 1956 Olympics. Egypt, Iraq, and Lebanon boycotted because of Egypt's battle with Israel, France, and Great Britain over which country should control the Suez Canal. And Spain, Switzerland, and the

Netherlands boycotted to protest developments in the communist country of Hungary. There, anti-communist demonstrations had led to a full-scale revolt by Hungarian citizens against the Soviet Union. The Soviets responded on November 4, 1956, with a massive invasion. The bombing of Budapest, Hungary's capital city, caused the deaths of 30,000 people. By then, athletes from both Hungary and the Soviet Union already had departed for the Olympics set to begin November 22nd in Australia. The hostilities between the nations would find new expression at the Melbourne Games.

On December 6, Hungary met the Soviet Union in the water polo competition. Hungary was the better team and was expected to win. As a supportive crowd cheered them on, the Hungarians built a 4-0 lead. Although there was elbowing and kicking throughout the match, most of it took place underwater, where the judges could not see. Then, with only a few minutes left, the game turned even more violent. After Hungary's Ervin Zador emerged from a confrontation with a bloody gash beneath his eye, angry fans rushed to the pool area, eager to pay the Soviets back for their aggression. As police quieted the crowd, officials called an end to the match and awarded the victory to Hungary. The team went on to win all seven of its matches and take the gold medal, while the Soviets ended up with the bronze. When the Olympics came to a close, 45 Hungarian athletes sought political asylum in Australia, refusing to return to their country as long as it was under Soviet rule.

Politics continued to infringe upon the Olympic Games in the 1960s, '70s, and '80s. The IOC banned South Africa from the Games from 1964 until 1991, when the country ended apartheid, its policy of segregation and racial discrimination against nonwhites.

HUNGARY'S ERVIN ZADOR WAS INJURED IN THE WATER POLO MATCH BETWEEN HIS COUNTRY AND THE SOVIET UNION AT THE 1956 OLYMPICS. HUNGARY WAS AHEAD 4-0 WHEN OFFICIALS CALLED THE GAME DUE TO EXCESSIVE VIOLENCE.

In 1972, the U.S. and Soviet Union paired off in one of the most controversial games in Olympic history. Stoked by the political rivalry between democracy and communism, the two teams met in the basketball final. Time expired with the U.S. ahead 50-49, but officials ruled that the Soviets had called a time-out before the final buzzer sounded. They first gave the Soviets one more second, then three more seconds. As the last second ticked away, the Soviets sank a layup, winning the game and the gold medal. The U.S. team appealed the decision, but a five-man jury, including three judges from communist countries—political allies of the Soviet Union—ruled that the Soviets had won. At the medal ceremony, the platform for the silver medalists remained empty. More than thirty years later, the Americans still have not claimed their medals.

THIS IMAGE OF A MASKED PALESTINIAN TERRORIST ON A BALCONY IN THE OLYMPIC VILLAGE IN MUNICH BECAME A SYMBOL OF THE BLEAKEST CHAPTER IN OLYMPIC HISTORY.

However, in 1968 an unauthorized Olympic protest by two Americans against racial discrimination was met with a harsh punishment. Tommie Smith had won the gold medal in the 200-meter sprint and John Carlos had won the bronze. While on the medal stand, they raised their fists in a silent Black Power salute (*see page 46*). This display, meant to quietly draw attention to discrimination faced by African Americans, was seen around the world on TV. IOC members were incensed that Smith and Carlos had used the Games to make a political statement. They ordered them out of the Olympic Village and banned them from future Olympiads. The IOC was determined to keep unauthorized political displays out of the Games. In 1972, it would learn how impossible that was.

Early in the morning on September 5, 1972, eight Palestinian terrorists sneaked into the Olympic Village in Munich, West Germany, and headed for the rooms of the team from Israel. Once there, they killed a wrestling coach and a weight lifter and took nine hostages. The terrorists demanded that Israel release 234 Arab prisoners and that the Germans provide the terrorists with safe passage out of the country.

After the captors transported the hostages to a nearby air base, German sharpshooters opened fire. In the fighting that followed, the terrorists killed all nine hostages. Five Palestinians and one German police officer also died. Although the Games were suspended and a memorial service was held, competition resumed after only 34 hours. Later, a Palestinian spokesman explained why the terrorists had chosen the Olympics for their attack. "Sport is the modern religion of the western world," he said. "So we decided to use the Olympics, the most sacred ceremony of this religion, to make the world pay attention to us."

Security was increased at the Olympics after 1972. For the rest of the century there was only one deadly incident, a bombing in a public park at the 1996 Games in Atlanta that killed one person. The bombing suspect, an

U.S. ROWERS MICHAEL PETERSON (FRONT) AND JONATHAN HOLLAND OBSERVE A MOMENT OF SILENCE BEFORE THEIR RACE ON JULY 27, 1996. EARLY THAT MORNING ONE WOMAN WAS KILLED AND MORE THAN 100 PEOPLE WERE INJURED WHEN A BOMB EXPLODED IN A DOWNTOWN ATLANTA PARK NEAR SEVERAL OLYMPIC VENUES.

American militant, was finally caught in 2003. Meanwhile, nations continued to boycott the Olympics for political reasons. In 1980, President Jimmy Carter threatened to keep American athletes home from the Moscow Olympics unless the Soviet Union withdrew from Afghanistan, which it had invaded in December 1979. The Soviets stayed in Afghanistan, and more than 60 nations joined the U.S. in the boycott. Four years later, the Soviet Union and 13 of its allies retaliated by boycotting the Los Angeles Games.

In the 1990s, though, the fall of communism in Eastern Europe led to a more peaceful era. The 1992 Games were the first ones since 1948 to go forward without a boycott. In the spirit of the times, the IOC launched the Olympic Truce Foundation, which aimed "to protect...the interests of the athletes and sport in general and to contribute to the search for peaceful and diplomatic solutions to the various conflicts around the world." It was a lofty goal, especially considering the new challenges that the world would face after September 11, 2001. But it was consistent with Pierre de Coubertin's original vision for the modern Olympics. "Olympism as the holder and distributor of social peace," wrote Coubertin in 1919, "this will be the final rung to climb."

When Esther Kim (right) gave up her spot on the 2000 U.S. tae kwon do team to Kay Poe (left), her injured friend and rival, her gesture caught the attention of Olympic officials. Top, the original Fair Play trophy, given to athletes who "regard fairness as more important than winning at all costs."

CHAPTER 5

Like Pierre de Coubertin, many of the athletes who competed in the Olympics over the years approached the Games with high ideals. Although they set their sights on winning their events, their vision was not blinded by their quest for gold. Such was the case with Esther Kim. In 2000, Kim was scheduled to meet her best friend, Kay Poe, in the finals of the U.S. Olympic trials in tae kwon do. Poe

UNLIKELY
HEROES

had already beaten Kim once in the round-robin tournament, but then Poe dislocated her kneecap. Because of that, Kim was sure to win the rematch and earn an automatic berth on the Olympic team. Instead of taking an easy victory, Kim forfeited the match to her injured friend. Poe would go to Sydney; Kim would stay home.

"I felt the right thing to do was to bow out," said Kim. "It was the only decision to be made." Her noble gesture received so much attention that Kim got to go to Australia anyway, as a guest of the International Olympic Committee. "To do something like that is just so impressive. It's beyond words," IOC vice president Anita DeFrantz told Kim. "What you've done is so important to all the Olympians of the world."

THIS PHOTOGRAPH, WHICH SHOWS GERMAN AND FRENCH ROWERS SHAKING HANDS AFTER A 1960 OLYMPIC RACE, WAS USED
TO ILLUSTRATE A 1999 ARTICLE ON "SPORTSMANSHIP AND THE OLYMPIC SPIRIT." WROTE AUTHOR ROBERT PRINGARBE,
"SHOWING SPORTSMANSHIP MEANS TRYING TO BE A GOOD PLAYER, BUT ABOVE ALL IT MEANS SUCCEEDING IN ALWAYS BEING
A FINE PLAYER...BEING LOYAL ON THE FIELD OF PLAY, RESPECTING THE RULES AND THE REFEREE, AND BEING MODEST IN
VICTORY AND [ACCEPTING] DEFEAT WITHOUT RESENTMENT, RECRIMINATION, OR ANGER."

What Kim had done was to remind Olympians, and everyone else, of one of the guiding principles of the Olympic Games: fair play. "Sport is not only physical performance," former IOC member Willi Daume once said. "It is also moral performance." Kim's selfless act was a reminder that for every breakthrough athlete whose Olympic performance helps to redefine the Games, there are thousands whose achievements are significant in other ways. It was a shining example of good sportsmanship.

"Sportsmanship is the willingness to go beyond what is expected, to offer the sport something more," said John Naber, winner of four gold medals and one silver in swimming at the 1976 Games. From 1996 to 2004, Naber was president of U.S. Olympians, an organization of athletes who competed in the Games. He warned that with financial rewards increasing for those who win gold medals, "victory at any cost is rapidly becoming a temptation too large to resist." But, he added, "the gold medal is meaningful only if earned fairly."

Those looking for examples of good sportsmanship at the Olympics can find them throughout the history of the Games. One of the first involved two Canadian runners in the controversial 800-meter race at the 1928 Olympics. Fanny "Bobbie" Rosenfeld had never run the 800 before, but she entered in order to encourage her teammate Jean Thompson, who was recovering from a leg injury. During the race, Thompson was jostled by another runner and became flustered. Rosenfeld saw it happen and ran up alongside her. She spoke to Thompson as they ran, encouraging her to shake it off and keep going. Rosenfeld "could easily have gone past her if she wanted to," remembered teammate Jane Bell, "but she just ran along beside her and wouldn't let her stop." Team manager Alexandrine Gibb said Rosenfeld "let Jean finish fourth, taking fifth for herself. In the annals of women's athletics, there is no finer deed than this."

Perhaps the most famous display of Olympic sportsmanship took place in 1936, when Jesse Owens of the U.S. was having trouble in the qualifying round of the long jump. Owens was the world record holder in the event, but he fouled twice by stepping over the starting line before jumping. He had one more chance to move on to the final round. As Owens waited his turn, he was approached by his toughest challenger, Luz Long.

IF NOT FOR THE ENCOURAGEMENT OF HER TEAMMATE FANNY "BOBBIE" ROSENFELD, CANADA'S JEAN THOMPSON (ABOVE) MIGHT NOT HAVE COMPLETED THE 800-METER RACE AT THE 1928 OLYMPICS. THOMPSON, WHO RAN DESPITE AN INJURY, FINISHED FOURTH.

Eric Moussambani of Equatorial Guinea swims alone in his qualifying heat in the 100-meter freestyle race at the Sydney Olympics. Moussambani, who had learned to swim only nine months before, finished the heat in 1 minute, 52.72 seconds, more than double the time of the eventual medal winners. But his refusal to quit won him many admirers.

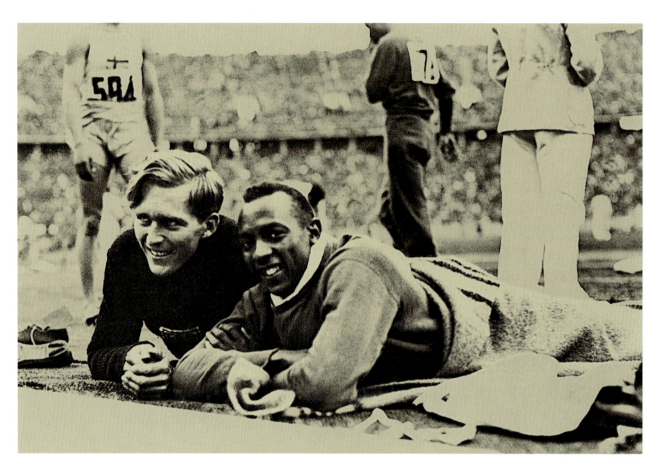

LUZ LONG (LEFT) AND JESSE OWENS WATCH THEIR COMPETITORS IN THE LONG JUMP AT THE 1936 SUMMER GAMES. OWENS WON THE GOLD MEDAL IN THE EVENT, THANKS TO A SUGGESTION BY LONG, WHO ENDED UP WITH THE SILVER. THE GERMAN THEN GAVE OWENS A HEARTY CONGRATULATIONS WITH ADOLF HITLER LOOKING ON.

The blond-haired, blue-eyed German suggested that Owens draw his own starting line a foot before the real one. He knew that the American was strong enough to qualify even if he took off early.

Owens followed Long's suggestion. He qualified for the final, where he and Long both broke the Olympic record as they pushed each other through the six-jump program. In the end, Owens won the gold medal, while Long took the silver. And despite German chancellor Adolf Hitler's attempts to belittle black athletes, Long and Owens became great friends. Long even wrote letters to Owens during World War II, when Long was serving as a soldier in the German army. Before he was killed in battle in 1943, Long included a request in one of his letters. "Someday find my son Karl," he wrote, "and tell him about his father." Several decades later, Owens went to meet Karl Long. When Karl got married, he turned to his father's friend Jesse Owens to serve as his best man.

As other athletes made their own sacrifices in international competition, officials sought ways to recognize their acts. In 1964, representatives of a number of sports organizations formed the International Fair Play Committee, which honors athletes with trophies and certificates. The first award went to Lars and Stig Kall of Sweden for a sacrifice they made at the 1964 Tokyo Olympics. The Swedish pair gave up their chance of winning the Flying Dutchman sailing competition when they stopped to help two other men whose boat had sunk. They ended up finishing 18th in a field of 21 teams.

Whether they win recognition or not, athletes who put fair play ahead of victory and keep going against all odds achieve one of the greatest benefits offered by sports, the experience of rising to a challenge. In some cases that means making sacrifices to help competitors in their time of need. In others it means pushing oneself to continue, despite physical pain or the knowledge that it is impossible to win. "That spirit of ambition and fair play is what allows all Olympians to feel like winners, if they just play by the rules, perform up to their potential, and try to win," John Naber wrote in the U.S. Olympians newsletter.

At the 2000 Summer Games, Eric Moussambani of Equatorial Guinea in Africa inspired everyone who watched him with his indomitable spirit. A wild-card entry in the 100-meter freestyle swimming race, Moussambani had taken up the sport only nine months before. Until he got to Sydney, he had never even practiced in a regulation 50-meter Olympic pool. On September 20, Moussambani was the only swimmer in his heat because the other two men had been disqualified. Gasping for air and nearly drowning throughout the second of two laps, he doggedly continued onward. He finished to a chorus of cheers, even though his time was more than double that of the fastest qualifier. Moussambani came away from his experience determined to find a coach and qualify for the 2004 Olympics. ESPN called him "the most unlikely hero of the Sydney Games."

Unlikely heroes such as Eric Moussambani, Esther Kim, "Bobbie" Rosenfeld, and Luz Long are the very people who ensure the future of the Olympic Games. They are the embodiment of the ideals that drove Pierre de Coubertin to resurrect the Games in 1896. For them, taking part was more important than winning and playing fair was more honorable than taking advantage of a competitor's weakness. As officials grapple with political controversies, drug violations, and other examples of what is wrong with the Olympic Games, they can look to these athletes for a reminder of what is right.

Pitcher ★ **LISA FERNANDEZ** ★ jumps for joy as the U.S. beats China to win the first ever gold medal in softball at the 1996 Olympics. The U.S. also would win Olympic Softball gold in 2000 and 2004.

★ **ANDRÉ NOYELLE** ★ of Belgium completes the 190.4-kilometer (118.3-mile) course to win the cycling road race at the 1952 Olympics in Helsinki. Noyelle beat his countryman Robert Grondelaers by 48 seconds.

2000 Olympic Gold Medal, Back

After winning the gold medal in the 200-meter butterfly at the 2000 Olympics, U.S. swimmer ★ **MISTY HYMAN** ★ (left) gets a hug from teammate ★ **KAITLIN SANDENO.** ★ Sandeno later won a bronze medal in the 800-meter freestyle event.

Track star ★ **KELLY HOLMES** ★ of Great Britain holds the British flag after winning the gold medal in the 1,500-meter race at the 2004 Summer Games. A few days earlier, Holmes also took the gold in the 800 meters.

Sweden's ★ **MIKAEL LJUNGBERG** ★ is thrilled after his victory over Davyd Saldadze of Ukraine nets him the gold medal in the 97-kilogram (214-pound) Greco-Roman wrestling event at the 2000 Summer Games.

★ **MARTY NOTHSTEIN** ★ of the United States raises his arms in victory as he receives his gold medal for the men's cycling sprint event at the 2000 Summer Games. Nothstein is flanked by silver medalist Florian Rousseau (right) of France and bronze medalist Jens Fiedler (left) of Germany.

2000 Olympic Gold Medal, Front

★ **LI XIAOPENG** ★ of China celebrates as he and his countrymen take the gold in the men's gymnastics team finals at the 2000 Sydney Games. China had won silver in the event at three of the previous four Olympics. This was their first ever team gymnastics gold.

PHOTO GALLERY

CELEBRATING

At the 2000 Summer Games, Russia's rhythmic gymnasts show off the gold medals they received for winning the team competition. Russia's ★ **YULIA BARSUKOVA** ★ (third from right) also earned the gold in the individual rhythmic all-around event.

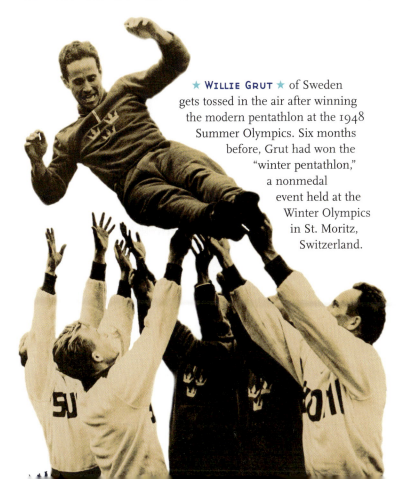

★ **WILLIE GRUT** ★ of Sweden gets tossed in the air after winning the modern pentathlon at the 1948 Summer Olympics. Six months before, Grut had won the "winter pentathlon," a nonmedal event held at the Winter Olympics in St. Moritz, Switzerland.

CANADA

Montréal 1976, XXI

UNITED
STATES

Los Angeles 1932, X
1984, XXIII

St. Louis 1904, III

Atlanta 1996, XXVI

MEXICO

Mexico City 1968, XIX

SWEDEN
Stockholm 1912, V
(Equestrian only) 1956, XVI

FINLAND
Helsinki 1952, XV

R U S S

Moscow 1980, XXII

UNITED KINGDOM
London 1908, IV
1948, XIV
2012, XXX

GERMANY
Berlin 1936, XI

Munich 1972, XX

NETHERLANDS
Amsterdam 1928, IX

GREECE
Athens 1896, I
2004, XXVIII

BELGIUM
Antwerp 1920, VII

SPAIN
Barcelona
1992, XXV

ITALY
Rome
1960, XVII

FRANCE
Paris 1900, II
1924, VIII

SUMMER OLYMPIC SITES

MAP KEY

■ Athens 1896, I ——— Roman numeral
given to competition

Site
of Games

Year they
took (will take) place

*Olympiads are numbered every four years
whether they take place or not. Games
VI (1916), XII (1940), and XIII (1944) were
canceled due to World Wars I and II.*

Present-day boundaries are shown.

I A

JAPAN

BEIJING 2008,
XXIX

Tokyo 1964, XVIII

CHINA

SOUTH KOREA
SEOUL 1988, XXIV

AUSTRALIA

SYDNEY 2000, XXVII

MELBOURNE 1956, XVI

OLYMPIC

ALMANAC

SUMMER OLYMPICS AT A GLANCE

No.	Year	Location	Nations	Sports	Events	Athletes	Male	Female
I	1896	ATHENS, GREECE	14	9	43	245	245	0
II	1900	PARIS, FRANCE	24	18	87	1,225	1,206	19
III	1904	ST. LOUIS, MISSOURI	13	17	94	689	681	8
IV	1908	LONDON, UNITED KINGDOM	22	22	109	2,035	1,999	36
V	1912	STOCKHOLM, SWEDEN	28	14	102	2,547	2,490	57
VI	1916	BERLIN, GERMANY			C A N C E L E D			
VII	1920	ANTWERP, BELGIUM	29	20	154	2,669	2,591	78
VIII	1924	PARIS, FRANCE	44	17	126	3,092	2,956	136
IX	1928	AMSTERDAM, NETHERLANDS	46	14	109	3,014	2,724	290
X	1932	LOS ANGELES, CALIFORNIA	37	14	116	1,408	1,281	127
XI	1936	BERLIN, GERMANY	49	19	129	4,066	3,738	328
XII	1940	TOKYO, JAPAN			C A N C E L E D			
XIII	1944	LONDON, UNITED KINGDOM			C A N C E L E D			
XIV	1948	LONDON, UNITED KINGDOM	59	17	136	4,099	3,714	385
XV	1952	HELSINKI, FINLAND	69	17	149	4,925	4,407	518
XVI	1956	MELBOURNE, AUSTRALIA*	72	17	151	3,342	2,958	384
XVII	1960	ROME, ITALY	83	17	150	5,348	4,738	610
XVIII	1964	TOKYO, JAPAN	93	19	163	5,140	4,457	683
XIX	1968	MEXICO CITY, MEXICO	112	20	172	5,530	4,750	780
XX	1972	MUNICH, WEST GERMANY	121	23	195	7,123	6,065	1,058
XXI	1976	MONTREAL, CANADA	92	21	198	6,028	4,781	1,247
XXII	1980	MOSCOW, USSR	80	21	203	5,217	4,093	1,124
XXIII	1984	LOS ANGELES, CALIFORNIA	140	23	221	6,797	5,230	1,567
XXIV	1988	SEOUL, SOUTH KOREA	159	25	237	8,465	6,279	2,186
XXV	1992	BARCELONA, SPAIN	169	28	257	9,367	6,659	2,708
XXVI	1996	ATLANTA, GEORGIA	197	26	271	10,320	6,797	3,523
XXVII	2000	SYDNEY, AUSTRALIA	199	28	300	10,651	6,582	4,069
XXVIII	2004	ATHENS, GREECE	201	28	301	10,625	6,296	4,329
XXIX	2008	BEIJING, CHINA		28	302			
XXX	2012	LONDON, UNITED KINGDOM		26				

*Equestrian events took place in Stockholm, Sweden. All totals include equestrian events and participants.

NOTE ON STATISTICS

OLYMPICS EXPERTS OFTEN DISAGREE on statistics that report the numbers of athletes and events at any given Summer Games. Dan Bell, a sports librarian and author of the *Encyclopedia of International Games,* says the reason is that at the earliest modern Olympics, exact records were not always kept. "We've been much more attuned in the last decade or two to the 'biggest, best, most' idea," says Bell, "so people started keeping more detailed records. I don't get the impression that it ever occurred to people at the earliest Olympic Games to be concerned with that."

As a result, record keepers were not consistent when they counted events and participants. For example, at some early Olympiads, events were canceled due to the weather or a lack of competitors. Did the canceled events count in the totals? Also, when the Olympics took place over a five-month span, some events were not even advertised as being part of the Games. Were they included in the count? And sometimes, nations sent athletes to the Olympics, but none of them competed. Should those athletes and nations be counted as participants?

Some historians have accepted the numbers given in the official report of each Olympiad, while others have revised those numbers after doing their own research. In putting together the "Summer Olympics at a Glance" chart, I used the statistics reported on the International Olympic Committee's official Web site, *www.olympics.org.* The only exception involves the 1956 totals, which were revised to include the equestrian events. The statistics here are closely matched in books by Bud Greenspan, Erich Kamper, and Bill Mallon, three of the leading authorities on the Olympic Games. The numbers of some other authorities differ, but not by much.

YOUNGEST, OLDEST RECORD-SETTERS

Age	Athlete	Achievement
10 years, 218 days	**Dimitrios Loundras** Greece Gymnast*	Probably the youngest athlete to compete at the Summer Games (team parallel bars, 1896)
12 years, 24 days	**Inge Sørensen** Denmark Swimmer	Youngest athlete to win a medal in an individual event (bronze, 200-meter breaststroke, 1936)
13 years, 268 days	**Marjorie Gestring** U.S. Diver	Youngest athlete to win a gold medal in an individual event (springboard diving, 1936)
14 years, 309 days	**Kusuo Kitamura** Japan Swimmer	Youngest male athlete to win a gold medal in an individual event (1,500-meter freestyle, 1932)
53 years, 277 days	**Sybil "Queenie" Newall** Great Britain Archer	Oldest female athlete to win a gold medal in an individual event (archery, 1908)
61 years, 4 days	**Joshua Millner** Great Britain Shooter	Oldest athlete to win a gold medal in an individual event (free rifle prone shooting event, 1908)
72 years, 279 days	**Oscar Swahn** Sweden Shooter	Oldest Olympic medalist ever (silver, double-shot running deer team shooting event, 1920)

MARJORIE GESTRING HUGS HER TRAINER AFTER WINNING OLYMPIC GOLD IN 1936.

OSCAR SWAHN, 1920

*Reports of a younger athlete who served as coxswain to the 1900 gold medal pair-oared shell rowing team have proved impossible to verify. Therefore, many people now consider Loundras to be the youngest Summer Olympian.

OLYMPIC SNAPSHOTS

Although the Summer Games share certain standards and traditions, every Olympiad has a flavor all its own. Here are some breakthroughs and highlights from each edition of the Summer Olympics.

100-Meter Sprint, 1896

Official Poster, 1900

1896
1st Olympiad
APRIL 6 TO APRIL 15
ATHENS, GREECE

Baron Pierre de Coubertin planned to stage the first modern Olympics in his home country of France in 1900. However, Greece was so enthusiastic about the rebirth of its ancient games that the IOC scheduled an earlier Olympics for that country. Athletes from 14 nations attended, most of them from Europe and all of them men. The U.S. team consisted largely of students from Princeton and Harvard who paid their own way.

First-place finishers received silver medals and crowns of olive branches, while runners-up won bronze medals and crowns of laurel. Among the most celebrated winners was Spiridon Loues. The Greek shepherd won the marathon in 2 hours, 58 minutes, 50 seconds. Only two of the other 16 entrants finished the 40,000-meter (24-mile, 4,514-feet) race. Legend has it that a Greek woman named Melpomene ran the race unofficially, finishing in four and a half hours.

1900
2nd Olympiad
MAY 14 TO OCTOBER 28
PARIS, FRANCE

After the success of the 1896 Olympics, some nations suggested that Athens be made the permanent home of the Games. But Baron de Coubertin was eager to present the second Olympiad in his home country as part of the 1900 Paris Exposition. He would regret his decision. Fair organizers downplayed the importance of the sporting events, scheduling them over a five-and-a-half-month period and failing to designate some of them as part of the Olympics. In fact, some athletes never knew they had competed in the Olympic Games. Historians consider these Games, and the ones in 1904, to be the least successful in modern times.

Still, there were memorable performances. U.S. star Alvin Kraenzlein won four individual gold medals in track and field, and American Ray Ewry won three jumping events. A small contingent of women also competed in golf, croquet, and tennis. Britain's Charlotte Cooper became the first female Olympic champion when she won the tennis tournament, and Margaret Abbott became the first female champion from the U.S. when she won in golf. Interestingly, the third-place finisher in tennis was an American who shared a name with the beleaguered track star of the 2000 Games, Marion Jones.

1904
3rd Olympiad
JULY 1 TO NOVEMBER 23
ST. LOUIS, MISSOURI

In St. Louis, the practice of receiving gold, silver, and bronze medals for first-, second-, and third-place finishes began. The St. Louis Games also saw the introduction of boxing and wrestling as Olympic sports, and the first African-American medalists: Joseph Stadler took a silver medal in the standing high jump and George Poage won bronze in the 400-meter hurdles.

Originally, the 1904 Olympics were awarded to Chicago. They were moved to St. Louis to be part of the World's Fair being held in that city. Unfortunately, the mistakes of the 1900 Games were repeated and the Olympic events were lost amid the chaos of the Fair. Events were scheduled over four and a half months, and few athletes from outside the United States took part. Among those who did compete were the first Olympic athletes from Africa, marathoners Len Tau and Jan Machiani, who were working at the World's Fair. Women competed only in archery, and their involvement was considered unofficial. Still, archer Lida Howell became the first American woman to win three gold medals when she took both individual events and shared in the team title.

OFFICIAL POSTER, 1904

BADGE FROM THE LOUISIANA PURCHASE EXPOSITION, SITE OF THE 1904 OLYMPIC GAMES

1906
Interim Games
APRIL 22 TO MAY 2
ATHENS, GREECE

Although they are not considered official Olympic Games, the 1906 Interim Games were crucial to the success of the Olympic movement. After the loosely run affairs in 1900 and 1904, organizers were desperate to revive their plans for an independent sports festival. To get things back on track, Greece volunteered to hold an Interim Olympics in 1906. Twenty countries sent a total of 884 athletes (877 men and 7 women) to Athens, and for the first time, the United States sent a formal national team. These Games also included the first opening ceremony, with athletes marching in by country behind their nation's flag.

1908
4th Olympiad
APRIL 27 TO OCTOBER 31
LONDON, UNITED KINGDOM

Originally scheduled to take place in Rome, the 1908 Games were moved to London at Italy's request. The volcano Mount Vesuvius had erupted in 1906, and Italy had to put all its resources into recovering from the damage. On short notice, London put together a well-organized Olympiad. New sports included diving, field hockey, and figure skating, which was part of the Summer Olympics until the Winter Games began in 1924. Women's events were added as an official part of the program for the first time, although the American Olympic Committee refused to send female athletes. It disapproved of the short skirts women wore in competition.

Queen Alexandra of England requested that the marathon begin at Windsor Castle, so her grandchildren could see the start of the race. The distance from the castle to the finish line at the Olympic Stadium, 26 miles, 385 yards, became the official length of a marathon. The race gave rise to the biggest controversy of the Games, when officials illegally picked up the exhausted leader, Italy's Dorando Pietri, and helped him toward the finish line. Pietri beat American Johnny Hayes by a few meters, but Hayes was declared the winner after a U.S. protest.

DORANDO PIETRI GETS SOME HELP AS HE CROSSES THE FINISH LINE IN THE 1908 OLYMPIC MARATHON.

The British had a special trophy made for Pietri, which was awarded to him by the Queen.

5th Olympiad
MAY 5 TO JULY 27
STOCKHOLM, SWEDEN

Stockholm built on the success of the London Games and delivered an Olympics that would serve as a model for the future. Improvements included the first public-address system and the unofficial use of electronic timing devices for some events. Women's swimming and diving contests were added to the program, as were equestrian (horseback riding) events and the unique five-part competition called the modern pentathlon. This competition combined shooting, swimming, fencing, horseback riding, and running, and until 1952 was always won by a military officer. In Stockholm, the top U.S. finisher was future World War II General George S. Patton, Jr., who came in fifth.

Finland's Hannes Kolehmainen won three gold medals and a silver in long-distance running, but Jim Thorpe of the U.S. was the breakout star of the 1912 Olympiad. Thorpe won the track and field pentathlon, which consisted of the long jump, the javelin and discus throws, the 200-meter run, and the 1,500-meter run. Then he won the decathlon, which included 10 running, jumping, and throwing events.

JIM THORPE, 1912

1916

6th Olympiad
CANCELED

Scheduled to take place in Berlin, Germany, the 1916 Olympic Games were canceled due to World War I. Following a practice of the ancient Greeks, the IOC decided to continue counting the canceled Games as the 6th Olympiad, and to label the 1920 Games the 7th Olympiad.

1920

7th Olympiad
APRIL 20 TO SEPTEMBER 12
ANTWERP, BELGIUM

Belgium suffered greatly during World War I, and the country was awarded the 1920 Olympic Games as a tribute to its people. The aggressor nations in the war, Germany, Austria, Turkey, Bulgaria, and Hungary, were not invited to attend. As a celebration of peace, white doves were released at the start of the Games. The Olympic flag was flown for the first time and the Athletes' Oath was introduced.

Despite the best efforts of the Belgian people, conditions at the Games were rough. Swimmers and divers competed in an outdoor pond with ice-cold murky water. Between events, some Americans traveled to nearby battlefields and picked up abandoned shells and helmets to take back home. Still, the Games saw a number of impressive performances. Finnish runner Paavo Nurmi made the first of his three Olympic appearances, winning three gold medals and a silver. This was also the first time the American team included a full contingent of women. Swimmer Ethelda Bleibtrey led the women by winning three gold medals, setting a world record in each of her events.

1924
8th Olympiad
MAY 4 TO JULY 27
PARIS, FRANCE

Pierre de Coubertin planned to retire from the IOC in 1925, and he was anxious to hold the Olympics in his home country before then. He got the chance in 1924. There were a number of firsts at the eighth Olympiad, including the introduction of the Olympic motto, *Citius, Altius, Fortius* (Latin for Swifter, Higher, Stronger). Five months before the Summer Games, the first Winter Olympiad was held in Chamonix, France.

Finland's Paavo Nurmi was the undisputed star of these Games, winning five gold medals, including two in the 1,500-meter and 5,000-meter races only about an hour apart. William DeHart Hubbard won the long jump to become the first African-American athlete to bring home the gold in an individual event. (John Baxter Taylor, Jr., had won gold in the 4 x 400-meter team relay in 1908.) U.S. swimmer and future star of the Tarzan movies, Johnny Weissmuller, won three gold medals and then earned a bronze with the U.S. water polo team. The U.S. women won four gold, three silver, and three bronze medals in the five swimming events on the program. New Yorker

U.S. SWIMMERS JOHNNY WEISSMULLER (LEFT) AND DUKE KAHANAMOKU, 1924

Gertrude Ederle took home two bronze medals and a gold. In 1926, she would become the first woman to swim across the English Channel.

1928
9th Olympiad
MAY 17 TO AUGUST 12
AMSTERDAM, THE NETHERLANDS

Two lasting traditions began at the Amsterdam Games. During the opening ceremonies, athletes from Greece marched into the stadium first, while those from the host country marched last. Then an Olympic flame was lit, to burn until the end of the Games. The ninth Olympiad also saw the first gold medalists from Asia: Japan's Mikio Oda won the triple jump, his countryman Yoshiyuki Tsuruta won the 200-meter breaststroke, and India won the first of six straight gold medals in field hockey. Finally in 1928, Finland's famed runner Paavo Nurmi returned to win one more gold and two more silver medals.

After almost a decade of lobbying by women's groups, the first women's track events were added to the program. But they were plagued by controversy. First the results were questioned when Betty Robinson of the U.S. narrowly beat Canada's Fanny "Bobbie" Rosenfeld in the 100-meter sprint. Then reporters and officials overreacted when some exhausted runners dropped to the ground at the end of the 800-meter race. Although Germany's Lina Radke won the event in world record time, critics claimed that women were too fragile to run "long" distances. The 800 would not return to the women's Olympic program until 1960.

1932
10th Olympiad
JULY 30 TO AUGUST 14
LOS ANGELES, CALIFORNIA

Los Angeles saw a number of innovations that would have a lasting impact on the Olympic Games. Automatic timing devices and photo-finish cameras were used for all track events. Medal winners stood on victory stands while their nations' flags were raised. Male athletes were housed in a single Olympic Village, though females stayed in a luxury hotel. And all of the events of the Olympics took

BETTY ROBINSON OF THE U.S., FIRST FEMALE OLYMPIC GOLD MEDALIST IN TRACK AND FIELD, 1928

OFFICIAL POSTER, 1928

place in a 16-day period, instead of spilling over three to six months as they had since the second Olympiad.

Although the Great Depression and the distance of Los Angeles from Europe kept the Games relatively small, 18 world records were either tied or broken in L.A. Three records were set by Texas phenom Mildred "Babe" Didrikson. She remains the only athlete in the history of the Olympics to win medals in separate throwing, running, and jumping events.

1936
11th Olympiad
AUGUST 1 TO AUGUST 16
BERLIN, GERMANY

Thirteen days before the beginning of the Berlin Olympics, the sun's rays were used to light a flame in Olympia, Greece. A torch bearing that flame was taken by a Greek runner. He delivered it to the next runner in a chain of 3,000 who eventually brought it to Berlin. This was the first Olympic torch relay, and it set the stage for the most controversial Summer Games to date. Germany's chancellor, Adolf Hitler, hoped to use the Olympics to prove his claims about the superior abilities of the blond-haired, blue-eyed Aryan race. But Jesse Owens helped to foil that plan.

Owens, the African-American track star, won four gold medals in Berlin, more than anyone else at the Games. His African-American teammates, Archie Williams, John Woodruff, and Cornelius Johnson, won three more. Although Hitler liked to congratulate gold medal winners, he skipped that practice with these Americans. But their successes were seen by a large audience. For the first time ever, the Olympics were shown on TV on 25 large, experimental sets in theaters throughout Berlin. The Games were also the subject of the first full-length official Olympic film—*Olympia,* directed by Leni Riefenstahl.

OFFICIAL POSTER, 1936

FILMING THE START OF A RACE FOR DIRECTOR LENI RIEFENSTAHL'S 1936 FILM, *OLYMPIA*

1940

12th Olympiad
CANCELED

Tokyo, Japan, was the site originally planned for the 1940 Summer Games, but in 1938, the Japanese government requested that a new location be chosen. Japan had been at war with China since 1937, and its leaders felt that the Olympics "could not be celebrated as they ought to be," according to the IOC. Helsinki, Finland, was chosen as the new site for 1940, but then the Games were canceled altogether due to World War II.

1944

13th Olympiad
CANCELED

London, England, beat out five other candidate cities for the 1944 Summer Games, but they were canceled due to World War II.

1948

14th Olympiad
JULY 29 TO AUGUST 14
LONDON, UNITED KINGDOM

With Great Britain still rebuilding after World War II, the 1948 Olympics were a no-frills affair. Reminders of German air raids were evident in London's battered landscape. Athletes stayed in army camps or remodeled schoolrooms, and luxury items were in short supply. Because they had been the aggressors in the war, Germany and Japan were banned from the Games. All in all, though, people saw the 14th Olympiad as an important step on the road back to normal life.

Outstanding performers included Fanny Blankers-Koen, who returned 12 years after her Olympic debut to win four gold medals in track and field for the Netherlands. American Bob Mathias won the decathlon only four months after taking up the event. U.S. high jumper Alice Coachman became the first African-American woman to bring home gold. Then there was Karoly Takács, a member of Hungary's pistol-shooting team. Ten years earlier, Takács had lost his right hand in a grenade explosion. He taught himself to shoot with his left hand and won the gold in the rapid-fire shooting event.

OFFICIAL POSTER, 1948

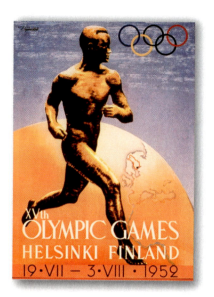

OFFICIAL POSTER, 1952

15th Olympiad

JULY 19 TO AUGUST 3
HELSINKI, FINLAND

Sweden set the standard for hosting a successful Olympics in 1912, and Finland built on that when the Games returned to Scandinavia in 1952. The well-staged festivities started with the lighting of the Olympic flame by Finland's two great runners, Paavo Nurmi and Hannes Kolehmainen. That set the stage for an extraordinary performance by another runner, Emil Zátopek of Czechoslovakia. In a span of eight days, Zátopek won the 10,000-meter race, the 5,000-meter race, and the marathon. His wife, Dana Zátopková, earned a gold medal of her own in the javelin throw.

These were the first Olympics in which a team from the Soviet Union competed, and the Soviet women were a force to reckon with in gymnastics and the throwing events of track and field. Another first involved the equestrian dressage event, which required a rider to direct a horse through a series of specific movements. In Helsinki, women competed directly against men in dressage for the first time, and they took the silver and bronze medals. The silver medalist, Lis Hartel of Denmark, won despite being paralyzed below the knees due to a bout with polio.

1956

16th Olympiad

NOVEMBER 22 TO DECEMBER 8
MELBOURNE, AUSTRALIA

Melbourne beat out Buenos Aires, Argentina, by only one vote to win the right to host the first Olympiad in the Southern Hemisphere. But Australia's laws required a long waiting period before animals could be brought into the country, so the equestrian events took place in Sweden. This was the only time a single Olympiad was held in two separate countries.

Just a month before the Games, the Soviet Union invaded Hungary to put down a revolt against communism. The political situation spilled over to the Olympics when Hungary met the Soviet Union in a violent water polo match that had to be stopped with Hungary ahead 4-0. In other sports, Hungarian athletes also stood tough. Gymnast Agnes Keleti won four gold and two silver medals and Laszlo Papp became the first boxer to win gold medals at three straight Olympics. In an optimistic end to a tense Olympiad, the athletes followed a suggestion by a young Australian boy named John Ian Wang. They marched into the closing ceremonies as a group, rather than by individual countries, beginning a practice that continues today.

1960

17th Olympiad
AUGUST 25 TO SEPTEMBER 11
ROME, ITALY

Once the site of ancient athletic contests, Rome staged the 1960 Games by combining a respect for the past with a celebration of the present. The wrestling and gymnastics events were held at locations that had hosted similar competitions 2,000 years before, while boxing, track and field, and cycling took place in brand-new facilities. For the first time ever, the Summer Games were broadcast around the world, live in Europe and on tape delay elsewhere.

With athletes from 83 nations now competing, a more diverse group of champions emerged. Abebe Bikila of Ethiopia became the first gold medalist from Africa when he won the marathon, and Germany's Armin Hary became the first winner of the 100-meter sprint who was not from an English-speaking country. U.S. winners included Wilma Rudolph, who brought home three gold medals in running events, and light heavyweight boxer Cassius Clay, who would later change his name to Muhammad Ali and become World Heavyweight champion. Following the Summer Olympics, Rome hosted the first Paralympics (short for "parallel Olympics") for athletes with disabilities. They continue to be held at the Olympic venues after each Summer and Winter Olympiad.

IN 1960, GERMANY'S INGRID KRÄMER WON GOLD IN BOTH SPRINGBOARD AND PLATFORM DIVING.

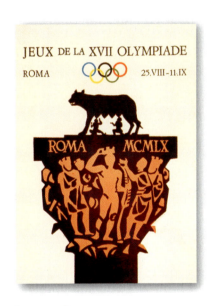

OFFICIAL POSTER, 1960

1964

18th Olympiad
OCTOBER 10 TO OCTOBER 24
TOKYO, JAPAN

Yoshinori Sakai was born August 6, 1945, in Hiroshima, Japan, the same day an atomic bomb exploded in the city. Nineteen years later, Sakai was chosen to light the Olympic flame during the opening ceremonies of the 18th Olympiad. The choice symbolized Japan's rebirth after its defeat in World War II. The athletes who traveled there for the first Summer Olympics in Asia found that the Japanese had spared no expense. They'd even built a new road system to handle traffic to and from the Games.

These Olympics saw the introduction of a judo competition for men and volleyball tournaments for men and women. Volleyball was the first team sport offered for women at the Olympics, and the gold medal went to the host country. Other noteworthy performers included Don Schollander of the U.S., who became the first swimmer to win four gold medals at a single Olympics. Australia's Dawn Fraser came back from a devastating car crash to win the 100-meter freestyle swimming race for the third straight time. Ethiopia's Abebe Bikila became the first man ever to win two straight Olympic marathons. And Larysa Latynina of the Soviet Union won her 17th and 18th medals in gymnastics. She remains the all-time female Olympic medal winner.

1968

19th Olympiad
OCTOBER 12 TO OCTOBER 27
MEXICO CITY, MEXICO

Mexico City was a controversial choice as a site for the Summer Olympics because it stands 7,546 feet (2,300 meters) above sea level. The air contains 30 percent less oxygen at that altitude than at sea level, causing endurance athletes to gasp for air during their races. That led to some disastrous results at the Olympics. One example: Australian Ron Clarke, who held the world record in the 10,000-meter run, collapsed at the end of his race and nearly died. On the other hand, athletes in jumping events and shorter races excelled. The long jump record of 29 feet,

2 1/2 inches (8.9 meters), set in Mexico City by Bob Beamon of the United States would stand for 22 years.

These were the first Summer Games to institute gender testing for women (*see Chapter Four*), and the first in which an athlete was disqualified for drug use. They were also the first Games in which the Olympic flame was lit by a woman, Mexican hurdler Enriqueta Basilio. Among the lasting athletic achievements was the introduction of a headfirst style in the high jump by Dick Fosbury of the U.S. He won the gold medal, and his "Fosbury flop" quickly became the style of choice for high jumpers.

1972
20th Olympiad
AUGUST 26 TO SEPTEMBER 11
MUNICH, WEST GERMANY

U.S. swimmer Mark Spitz won seven gold medals, and Soviet gymnast Olga Korbut won three, but the 1972 Summer Games are remembered first and foremost for an act of terrorism. On September 5, eight Palestinian terrorists killed two members of the Israeli Olympic team and took nine hostages. When the terrorists tried to escape by plane from a nearby airport, all nine hostages, five terrorists, and one police officer were killed. Officials halted the Games for 34 hours in memory of the athletes who had died. Competition resumed after incoming IOC president Avery Brundage declared, "We cannot allow a handful of terrorists to destroy...the Olympic movement."

These Summer Games saw the return of competition in archery after 52 years and team handball after 36 years. Waldi the Dachshund became the first mascot at a Summer Olympics. Olympic officials also took an oath for the first time, promising to officiate "with complete impartiality...in the true spirit of sportsmanship." Yet the fairness of the judges came into question in the highly charged gold medal basketball game. The Soviet Union was given extra time twice after the buzzer sounded at the end of the game. The Soviets finally won, breaking the U.S. streak of seven gold medals in the sport.

OFFICIAL POSTER, 1972

OFFICIAL POSTER, 1980

MISHA THE BEAR, 1980
OLYMPIC MASCOT

1976
21st Olympiad
July 17 to August 1
MONTREAL, CANADA

After the tragedy of 1972, Montreal put on a safe, well-run 21st Olympiad, although financial problems led the Games to lose almost one billion dollars (Canadian). Still, the competition was memorable. Romanian gymnast Nadia Comaneci took her sport to a new level when she scored seven perfect tens and won three gold medals, one silver, and one bronze. Comaneci later said she was confused when she received her first 10. Since the electric scoreboard was only set to go as high as 9.99, her score came up as 1.0. It wasn't until people started cheering that she realized it was a 10.

Other 1976 highlights included the introduction of women's basketball, rowing, and team handball, and the domination of the men's swimming competition by the United States—American men took the gold in 12 of the 13 events. On the women's side, East Germany's swimmers won 11 of the 13 gold medals. Years later, the East Germans would admit that their female swimmers were given steroids to improve their performances.

1980
22nd Olympiad
JULY 19 TO AUGUST 3
MOSCOW, USSR

In December 1979, the Soviet Union invaded Afghanistan. U.S. President Jimmy Carter threatened to boycott the 1980 Moscow Olympics unless they withdrew. The Soviets stood tough, and so did Carter. Despite passionate protests by U.S. athletes, the President forbade American competitors to attend the Games. More than 60 other nations also kept their athletes home, among them Canada, West Germany, China, and Japan.

As a result, the Soviet Union and East Germany won nearly half of the 631 medals awarded in Moscow. Every one of the 54 East German rowers went home with a medal, and Soviet gymnast Aleksandr Dityatin earned a medal in every gymnastics event. Dityatin won three gold medals, four silver, and one bronze to become the first athlete ever to win eight medals at a single Olympics. Another unlikely achievement took place in the new Olympic sport of women's field hockey. Tournament organizers scrambled to find competitors after five of the six qualifying teams withdrew because of the boycott. Zimbabwe put together a team less than a week before the Olympics and won the gold medal.

1984
23rd Olympiad
JULY 28 TO AUGUST 12
LOS ANGELES, CALIFORNIA

Los Angeles was the only city to bid for the 1984 Summer Olympics, and the committee that planned the Games was determined to make them safe and profitable. Its first challenge was to overcome the effects of a boycott by the Soviet Union and 13 other countries, payback for the 1980 boycott led by the U.S. The Soviet boycott drained weight lifting, gymnastics, freestyle wrestling, and several other sports of their strongest competitors. But new stars emerged.

In track and field, American Carl Lewis matched Jesse Owens by taking gold in the 100-meter and 200-meter sprints, the long jump, and as part of the 4 x 100-meter relay team. Morocco's Nawal El Moutawakel became the first woman from an Islamic country to earn a gold medal when she won the 400-meter hurdles. In gymnastics, crowd favorite Mary Lou Retton became the first U.S. athlete ever to win the all-around individual gold medal. Connie Carpenter-Phinney of the U.S. won the first ever women's cycling road race and American Joan Benoit won the first women's marathon. In the end, the 1984 Games made a profit of $223 million. Most of the money went to support youth sports programs in the U.S. or to help pay the expenses of nations that had competed in L.A.

SAM THE EAGLE, 1984
OLYMPIC MASCOT

Florence Griffith Joyner
(FloJo), 1988

24th Olympiad
SEPTEMBER 17 TO OCTOBER 2
SEOUL, SOUTH KOREA

When the Summer Olympics traveled to Asia for the second time, the world witnessed some spectacular performances. Among them: Tennis was back at the Olympics after a 64-year absence, and West Germany's Steffi Graf capped a Grand Slam year by taking the gold. In track, Florence Griffith Joyner of the U.S. won three gold medals and a silver, setting a world record in the 200-meter dash that stood into the new millennium. And East Germany's Christa Luding-Rothenburger became the only person ever to win medals at the Winter and Summer Olympics in the same year. She added a silver in cycling to the gold and silver she had won in speed skating at the 1988 Winter Games.

On the other hand, Canada's Ben Johnson, winner of the 100-meter sprint, tested positive for steroids and was disqualified. And the world felt Greg Louganis's pain when the American smacked his head on the board in the qualifying rounds of the springboard diving competition. Louganis received stitches and returned 35 minutes later to continue diving. He ended up repeating as a gold medalist in both the springboard and the platform diving contests.

1992

25th Olympiad
JULY 25 TO AUGUST 9
BARCELONA, SPAIN

Between 1988 and 1992, major political changes took place in Europe and around the world. The Soviet Union broke into 15 separate countries; East and West Germany united; and South Africa denounced apartheid. As a result of this new world order, there were no boycotts at the 25th Olympiad, and more nations and athletes took part than ever before.

Against that backdrop, athletes from all parts of the globe had the chance to shine. Gymnast Vitaly Scherbo of Belarus won six gold medals, four of them in a single day. Jackie Joyner-Kersee of the U.S. won her second straight heptathlon gold, as well as a bronze in the long jump. China's Zhang Shan became the first female athlete to win a shooting contest open to both men and women when she took the gold in skeet shooting. The U.S. men's basketball "Dream Team," which included pros from the NBA, won all eight of its games and scored an average of 117 points on the way to gold. And Derartu Tulu of Ethiopia became the first black woman from Africa to capture a gold medal when she won the 10,000-meter race. Tulu's victory lap with silver medalist Elana Meyer, a white South African, seemed a reminder of how the world had changed.

1996

26th Olympiad
JULY 19 TO AUGUST 4
ATLANTA, GEORGIA

During the summer of 1996, news magazines summarized the 26th Olympiad with a single phrase: "triumph and terror." On the playing fields of Atlanta, athletes competed in 26 sports, including for the first time, beach volleyball, mountain biking, and women's soccer and softball. But early on the morning of July 27, a bomb went off in a park near the Olympic venues, killing one person and injuring more than a hundred. Fearing additional violence, athletes and spectators kept a watchful eye. Fortunately, no other bombings took place.

There were plenty of triumphs in Atlanta, too. Carl Lewis won the long jump for the fourth straight time. The U.S. women took gold in basketball, softball, and soccer and also won their first team gymnastics competition. Marie-José Pérec of France won the 200-meter and the 400-meter track races on the women's side, and Michael Johnson of the U.S. won them both on the men's side. And Austria's Hubert Raudaschl became the first person ever to take part in nine Olympiads. Twice a silver medalist, the yachtsman competed in every Olympics from 1964 through 1996. He had been an alternate for the 1960 Games.

TWO SIDES OF THE 1996
OLYMPIC GOLD MEDAL

RULON GARDNER (LEFT) IN ACTION
AGAINST ALEKSANDR KARELIN, 2000

HICHAM EL GUERROUJ WITH THE
MOROCCAN FLAG, 2004

2000
27th Olympiad
SEPTEMBER 15 TO OCTOBER 1
SYDNEY, AUSTRALIA

Australia's second staging of the Summer Games was full of good will and impressive achievements, although there were drug scandals as well. In gymnastics, Romania's Andreea Raducan won the individual all-around gold, only to have it taken away after she tested positive for a banned substance. U.S. shot putter C.J. Hunter, husband of track star Marion Jones, was forced to withdraw from the Games after he failed a drug test for steroids. In 2007, Jones would admit that she, too, had taken performance-enhancing drugs before the 2000 Games. With that admission, she surrendered the three gold and two bronze medals she won in Sydney.

Among the most successful athletes were U.S. veteran swimmers Dara Torres and Jenny Thompson, who won nine medals between them, and Australia's teenaged sensation Ian Thorpe, who swam to three gold medals and two silvers. U.S. Greco-Roman wrestler Rulon Gardner upset Russia's Aleksandr Karelin, who had won the super heavyweight title at three straight Olympics. The U.S. women's softball team came back from the brink of defeat to defend its gold medal, and the U.S. baseball team beat Cuba to win gold behind former L.A. Dodgers manager Tommy Lasorda. And unlike the 1956 Games, the equestrian events did take place in Australia. Germany won the team dressage and show jumping contests, while Australia won the team three-day event.

2004
28th Olympiad
AUGUST 13 TO AUGUST 29
ATHENS, GREECE

With their return to Athens in 2004, the Olympic Games had come full circle after 108 years of growth and change. This Olympiad saw women compete in almost every sport that men did, including wrestling for the first time. Women's teams from the U.S. clinched their third straight gold medals in softball and basketball and regained the title in soccer after losing in the final at Sydney. German kayaker Birgit

Fischer, an Olympian since 1980, won gold and silver medals and became the first woman in any sport to win gold medals at six different Olympiads.

U.S. swimmer Michael Phelps won six gold and two bronze medals to become only the second athlete to win eight medals at a single Summer Games. Meanwhile, South Africa took the gold in the 4 x 100-meter freestyle relay, its first medal ever in men's swimming. Runner Hicham El Guerrouj of Morocco won both the 1,500-meter and the 5,000-meter races, duplicating the feat of Paavo Nurmi in 1924. And despite the ongoing war at home, the Iraqi men's soccer squad upset several teams to finish just out of medal contention.

2008

29th Olympiad
AUGUST 8 TO AUGUST 24
BEIJING, CHINA

Several new events will be on the program when the world's athletes gather in China in 2008, led by men's and women's bicycle motocross (BMX), a new discipline in cycling. Other first-time contests will include women's foil and saber team events in fencing, men's and women's 10-kilometer events in swimming, the women's 3,000-meter steeplechase in track and field, and men's and women's team events in table tennis, which will replace the doubles competition.

2012

30th Olympiad
JULY 27 TO AUGUST 12
LONDON, UNITED KINGDOM

Baseball and softball will not be contested when the Summer Games return to London in 2012. The IOC voted to eliminate both sports from the program. Major League Baseball's refusal to allow its top stars to play at the Olympics seemed to be one strike against the sport. IOC president Jacques Rogge also complained that the major leagues did not do enough in the past to fight doping. The U.S. dominance in softball—the Americans outscored opponents 51-1 in 2004 on the way to the gold—seemed to move some European IOC members to vote against that sport. The IOC will consider restoring baseball and softball to the 2016 Olympics at a meeting in 2009.

WORKERS HANG A BILLBOARD FOR THE 2008 BEIJING OLYMPIC GAMES.

COMING SOON!

2010

1st Summer Youth Olympic Games

On July 5, 2007, IOC president Jacques Rogge announced plans for a 12-day, multi-sport competition for athletes ages 14 to 18 called the Youth Olympic Games. The Summer edition will premiere in 2010 and return every four years after that. In 2010, some 3,500 athletes from as many as 205 nations will compete in 26 different sports. Said Rogge, "Our hope is that if young people can learn to respect each other on the field of play, they may transfer this to the other parts of their daily lives."

RESEARCH NOTE

RESEARCHING A BOOK IS A COMPLETELY different experience in the Internet Age than it was before writers had a world of information at their fingertips. Still, I started the research for *Swifter, Higher, Stronger* the old-fashioned way, with a trip to the library. It was a very special library, to be sure, that of the LA84 Foundation. This non-profit organization, formerly known as the Amateur Athletic Foundation of Los Angeles, was the beneficiary of some of the profits from the 1984 Summer Olympics in L.A. Besides giving back to the community by funding sports programs for kids, the LA84 Foundation operates the Paul Ziffren Sports Resource Center, the largest sports research library in North America.

For someone who writes about sports history, visiting the LA84 Foundation's library is better than a trip to a candy store. There are floor-to-ceiling bookcases packed with just about every sports book ever written in the English language, plus bound volumes of magazines dating back to the turn of the 20th century. I spent the better part of a week there, and I didn't even enter the viewing room to examine their video collection of historic sports events. Instead, I dedicated most of my time to reading hard-to-find books, magazines, and microfilm, poring through the photo collection, and speaking with the expert staff.

When I finally left the warmth of Southern California and returned to the snow-covered winter bleakness of my Northern New Jersey home, I could still take advantage of many of the LA84 Foundation's resources. Their Web site, *www.la84foundation.org,* includes a virtual archive of reproductions, as Portable Document Format (PDF) files, of hundreds of issues of scholarly journals and significant documents related to the Olympics. Not the least of these is John J. MacAloon's 1981 book, *This Great Symbol: Pierre de Coubertin and the Origins of the Modern Olympic Games.* MacAloon's detailed academic account of Coubertin's life and ideas was an important source for the first chapter of this book.

Another indispensable resource is David Wallechinsky's *The Complete Book of the Summer Olympics,* published every four years. One of the world's premier Olympic historians, Wallechinsky has put together the results of every event in every sport starting in 1896. But this tightly packed volume is much more than a record book. The author includes anecdotes about many of the memorable Olympic contests of the past and many of the athletes whose names grace the medal lists.

When it came to finding personal details about the hundreds of Olympic athletes mentioned in this book, the Internet really made the difference. Established sports sites such as *www.ESPN.com* and *www.CNNSI.com* offer profiles of scores of accomplished Olympians, and official sites such as the IOC's *www.olympic.org* and the U.S. Olympic Committee's *www.usolympicteam.com* include terrific features on the Games and the athletes who've played them. But with "Google" at the ready, I often searched the vast expanse of the World Wide Web to find athletes' records, or the spelling of their names, or their reflections on their own Olympic experience. Google brought me to sites run by sports federations and small-town newspapers, sports fans, and even the Brisbane, Australia, city council (for a student paper on the participation of women in the 1928 Games). As always, it is important to take into consideration the bias of a particular site, and to double- and triple-check "facts" that seem questionable. If you have a question about the source of any fact or quotation in this book, or want further information about my research process, feel free to e-mail me at sue@suemacy.com.

Photo research, too, has been completely transformed now that photo agencies and museums have digitized their images and made them available to Internet researchers. Thanks to the technology of Corbis, Getty, AP/Wide World, and other organizations in Canada and Europe, I was able to find most of the pictures for this book without leaving home. The International Olympic Committee also came through with images from their unique collection, sent to us via e-mail. Although I miss the days of discovering eye-opening images crammed into file cabinets in the back rooms of photo archives, there's no denying that time spent photo researching today is more productive and possibly even has better results. That is for the readers of this book to decide.

RESOURCES

BOOKS

Carlson, Lewis H. and Fogarty, John J. *Tales of Gold: An Oral History of the Summer Olympic Games Told by America's Gold Medal Winners.* CHICAGO: CONTEMPORARY BOOKS, 1987.

Gold medalists from 1912 through 1984 remember their Olympic experiences and share their personal insights on sports, competition, and the Olympic movement.

Greenspan, Bud. *100 Greatest Moments in Olympic History.* LOS ANGELES: GENERAL PUBLISHING GROUP, INC., 1995.

Greenspan is a renowned journalist and filmmaker who ESPN says "is as much a part of the Olympics as the rings." Here, he presents a collection of profiles of athletes from around the world who made their mark during the first century of the Olympic Games.

Wallechinsky, David. *The Complete Book of the Summer Olympics.* TORONTO: SPORTCLASSIC BOOKS, 2004.

Simply the most comprehensive single volume on the Summer Games. Look for new editions to be published in each Olympic year.

WEB SITES

Association of Summer Olympic International Federations
www.asoif.com

On this site, you'll find links to 28 international federations that represent sports in the Summer Games. Each federation includes detailed background information on the sport and its rules, as well as up-to-the-minute news of athletes and competitions.

International Olympic Committee
www.olympic.org

Visit the "official Web site of the Olympic movement," to discover a wealth of information on the Summer and Winter Games including athlete profiles, highlights from each edition of the Olympics, news, and a large section on the history and current affairs of the IOC. There's also a link to the site of the Olympic Museum in Lausanne, Switzerland.

LA84 Foundation
www.la84foundation.org

Besides offering a beautiful online exhibit of art and posters from the Olympics, this site has a rich archive of sports material, including many oral histories and PDF files of the official reports from every Olympiad.

United States Olympic Committee
www.usolympicteam.com

Here you can find the name and event of every man and woman who has represented the United States at the Olympics since 1896. There's also lots of information about current athletes and upcoming Olympiads, as well as free videos and desktop wallpaper showing top Olympic stars.

VIDEOS

America's Greatest Olympians and *100 Years of Olympic Glory*, TURNER HOME VIDEO, 1996.

Two of the many films directed by Bud Greenspan, these were issued in conjunction with the 100th anniversary of the modern Olympics and highlight many inspiring athletes and memorable moments.

The First Olympics—Athens 1896, COLUMBIA TRISTAR HOME VIDEO, 1984.

An entertaining dramatization of the first modern Olympics, originally shown as a TV miniseries when the Games were held in Los Angeles in 1984. It's fun to see French actor Louis Jourdan as Pierre de Coubertin and other performers playing Robert Garrett, Spiridon Loues, and their fellow athletes from 1896.

INDEX

PICTURE CREDITS

One of the world's largest nonprofit scientific and educational organizations, the National Geographic Society was founded in 1888 "for the increase and diffusion of geographic knowledge." Fulfilling this mission, the Society educates and inspires millions every day through its magazines, books, television programs, videos, maps and atlases, research grants, the National Geographic Bee, teacher workshops, and innovative classroom materials. The Society is supported through membership dues, charitable gifts, and income from the sale of its educational products. This support is vital to National Geographic's mission to increase global understanding and promote conservation of our planet through exploration, research, and education.

For more information, please call 1-800-NGS-LINE (647-5463) or write to the following address: National Geographic Society 1145 17th Street, N.W. Washington, D.C. 20036-4688 U.S.A.

Visit the Society's Web site: www.nationalgeographic.com

PUBLISHED BY THE NATIONAL GEOGRAPHIC SOCIETY

John M. Fahey, Jr., *President and Chief Executive Officer*

Gilbert M. Grosvenor, *Chairman of the Board*

Tim T. Kelly, President, *Global Media Group*

Nina D. Hoffman, *Executive Vice President; President, Book Publishing Group*

STAFF FOR THIS BOOK

Nancy Laties Feresten, *Vice President, Editor-in-Chief of Children's Books*

Bea Jackson, *Design Director, Children's Books*

Jennifer Emmett, *Project Editor*

Marty Ittner, *Designer*

Lori Epstein, *Illustrations Editor*

Janet Dustin, *Illustrations Coordinator*

Carl Mehler, *Director of Maps*

Matt Chwastyk, *Map Production*

Mark A. Wentling, Connie D. Binder *Indexing*

R. Gary Colbert, *Production Director*

Lewis R. Bassford, *Production Manager*

Vincent P. Ryan, Nicole Elliot, *Manufacturing Managers*